Psychoeducational Evaluation of the Preschool Child

A Manual Utilizing the Haeussermann Approach

Eleonora Jedrysek, Dipl. Psychol. (Sorbonne), Psychologist, Children's Evaluation and Rehabilitation Center, Rose F. Kennedy Center, Albert Einstein College of Medicine, Bronx, New York

Lillie Pope, Ph.D., Director, Psycho-Educational Service, Department of Psychiatry, Coney Island Hospital, Brooklyn, New York

Zelda Klapper, Ph.D., Chief, Psychological Services, Children's Evaluation and Rehabilitation Center, Rose F. Kennedy Center, Albert Einstein College of Medicine, Bronx, New York

Joseph Wortis, M.D., Director, Developmental Center, Department of Psychiatry, Maimonides Medical Center, Brooklyn, New York

Psychoeducational Evaluation of the Preschool Child

A Manual Utilizing the Haeussermann Approach

Eleonora Jedrysek

Zelda Klapper

Lillie Pope

Joseph Wortis

With a Foreword by Else Haeussermann

Grune & Stratton

New York and London

Grune & Stratton, Inc.
111 Fifth Avenue
New York, New York 10003

Library of Congress Catalog Card Number 75-168848
International Standard Book Number 0-8089-0735-2
Printed in the United States of America

3/16/73 Rel. 8.95

Contents

Foreword

It has always been my conviction that the same careful analysis and evaluation given the handicapped preschool child should be equally available to the nonhandicapped child. During my early years as a social worker in Germany after World War I, as well as during the years spent in a public school in New York where the Cerebral Palsy classes were located, I frequently observed the inadequate functioning of some of the apparently average children. The desire to study them, beyond the findings revealed by the medical examination by the school physician, was great, especially when I could spot in such little school children many of the same distress signals that could be observed in our cerebral palsied population: It might be an immature manner of descending stairs, a consistent mispronunciation of certain unvoiced sounds, a squint of one eye on visual effort, or some other deficit.

It is therefore a great satisfaction to me that in this manual for the psychoeducational and developmental evaluation of the preschool child the philosophy, the approaches, and some of the materials I have used could be utilized. I had counted in decades rather than in years when dreaming of the realization of such opportunities for the normal child. The coming of the Headstart Program, attempts such as television's Sesame Street, probably together with the general dismay about school achievement across the country, seem to have accelerated the pace of history, and I am glad.

It was back in 1946 (after another World War), when I had returned to New York from Dr. Earl Carlson's School and from my own small kindergarten for cerebral palsied children in Albany and began to serve as kindergarten teacher and coordinator at the Cerebral Palsy Unit (started by the New York Service for Orthopedically Handicapped), that I began to search for help in organizing the Test Items which I had been employing tentatively and empirically in my work with cerebral palsied children. After sifting the available literature at Teachers College and Columbia University's Psychology Department, I came upon the papers written by Dr. Heinz Werner, who, with Dr. Alfred Strauss, had been working with neurologically impaired children at Wayne University. Gradually I found my way to Dr. Werner, who by then was at Brooklyn College. I told him that what was needed was a way to test cerebral palsied children. We discussed the difference between the neurologically impaired, with whom he and Strauss were concerned, and the cerebral palsied with whom I was concerned. Then came the memorable day when Dr. Werner visited our Cerebral Palsy Unit, then at the Lower East Side Health Center, and brought with him his "best assistant," Dr. Zelda Klapper (then Dr. Sobel).

Dr. Werner claimed to be too old to start on a task of this nature, and therefore he let me and Dr. Klapper use some of his original testing materials on the cerebral palsied child population of the C.P. Clinic at the Hospital for Special Surgery. In 1947 and in 1949, during two summer vacations, the late Dr. William Cooper, then Director of the C.P. Clinic as well as of our C.P. Unit, let us use the Clinic's space and its widely varied child population (including some polio patients) to arrive at some comparative data on the responses to the Items, Dr. Werner's as well as mine.

Thus it is with gratitude, confidence, and respect that I regard this manual. In reading it through, I frequently found myself back at those rooms at the C.P. Clinic in those exciting early days, trying out Items, thinking up new ones stemming from the narrow environment of the chairbound child and likely to elicit responses from children with the physical impediments found in cerebral palsy. The task of the present manual could not have been placed in more suitable hands. Dr. Klapper was an early associate; Dr. Wortis, Mrs. Jedrysek, and Dr. Pope have shared so many full years with me that they are actually part of both projects, my book on *Developmental Potential of Preschool Children* as well as the present manual. At the brief visits and short work conferences in Germany with Dr. Rosenblatt, Dr. Klapper, and Dr. Pope, as well as Dr. and Mrs. Wortis, and during the years as work went on in Brooklyn and New York in developing the manual, I was made to feel still part of the team and I was kept abreast of both the labors and the progress. It is a most gratifying experience for a retired worker to learn that former co-workers still carry on the work that was so very important to her.

This manual is based upon an awareness of the gross and subtle deficits found in preschool children in all areas of functioning needed for learning; it carefully describes Probes for the child who fails a Test Item expected at his level, gives the conscientious teacher a tool to spot the suspected trouble area, and frequently suggests approaches to remedial management for use in the classroom.

For the teachers and others concerned with preschool children, I believe the manual will bring the help which I and my fellow teachers, of nonhandicapped and handicapped children alike, have frequently missed so terribly when we wanted to help a child whose trouble we could sense, but could not pinpoint and define.

Else Haeussermann

x

Preface

Since this manual represents an extension and elaboration of Else Haeussermann's work it may be helpful to recall her own approach to the problem of developmental evaluation. She wanted to test children, particularly those with multiple handicaps, to find out how to teach them, and she taught them while studying and observing their qualities and capacities. She sought to bypass sensory or motor handicaps to discover what a child was really capable of, and to describe and analyze what she found without regard to rank order among peers or other statistical considerations.

Certain concerns which test constructors usually have were not part of her interest. While she was working with us she abandoned the ambition to develop a conventional test standardization that would yield a normal score distribution on a large population. She was convinced that when one dealt with the individual child, the important thing was to be able to describe the child; teachers were very eager to get her reports because, unlike the usual psychometric tests, they were of great practical help to them in working with the children.

Else Haeussermann began to develop her testing techniques many years ago when the first special class for the cerebral palsied was opened in the New York City schools. When the class was taken over by the public school system about 1955, Else moved to my former clinic, the Division of Pediatric Psychiatry in Jewish Hospital of Brooklyn. As her work developed and began to be widely known, it became apparent that what might lead to a unique product under Else's hands had to be used in a uniform way by others if the results of the testing experience were to be correctly understood and communicated.

And so in 1964 a new stage of the work was initiated with her blessing, though not with her full involvement, when we started, with support from the National Institute of Child Health and Human Development (NICHHD Grant PO1 HD01095), a project aimed at the extension and further development of the test. In the course of this work we tried to detail consistent procedures that would permit a certain amount of uniformity in the way the test was administered, and to make the procedures applicable to normal populations.

Some of our findings related to social class in a population of a few hundred children will be found in the paper by Jedrysek, Rosenblatt, and Wortis entitled "Social Class Influences on Intellectual Development" published in 1967 in the *Proceedings of the First Congress of the International Association for the Scientific Study of Mental Deficiency*. The present manual attempts to simplify the testing procedures and to make them more explicit. To adapt the Haeussermann materials to wider use, particularly by teachers of non-handicapped children, additional tests were included and test procedures were revised. Though the manual is written with the assumption that the examiner, whether teacher, psychologist, nurse, or whatever, will confront the child in a one-to-one relationship, the method also lends itself to classroom or playroom use and to systematic observation of the child in the course of group activities.

All the authors of this manual have been co-workers with Else Haeussermann. In the early years of her work Zelda Klapper was an associate. When the NICHHD project was funded the first participants included Else Haeussermann, Gilda Guzman, Eleonora Jedrysek, and Jay Rosenblatt, but Else retired and returned to Europe soon after the project began. After 1967 the project was transferred to the Developmental Center, Maimonides Medical Center, in Brooklyn, with the continued participation of Dr. Guzman and Mrs. Jedrysek, with support from the same source. A workshop on the Haeussermann Developmental Evaluation was held under the sponsorship of the Special Education Department of Teachers College of Columbia University on March 8 and 9, 1968, with 23 participants, most of whom had intimate knowledge of the procedure. The proceedings of the conference have been recorded. The idea for the manual was first proposed by Dr. Lillie Pope, also a former associate of Miss Haeussermann's in my clinic, in the course of this workshop, and the task of preparing such a manual was assumed with the continued support of NICHHD. Else, though far away, encouraged the work, reviewed the manuscript and met several of us in Europe to discuss some of its details. We hope it proves to be useful to others in the field.

One cautionary note should be added: This manual is essentially psychological and educational in its orientation and interest. But problems of human development always implicate nonpsychological aspects: the biological intactness or condition of the organism, fatigue or alertness, efficiency and integration of specific sensory modalities, motor capac-

ity or disability, the harmful or helpful influence of drugs, etc. As a physician I should perhaps emphasize that the omission of these considerations in this manual does not mean they are unimportant. On the contrary, the observant teacher or psychologist should be alert to these dimensions and seek help when necessary. Unfortunately many biological impairments are too slight or subtle to be diagnosed by conventional medical techniques, and there is a widespread but mistaken belief that a routine medical examination can exclude the possibility of a physical-biological-physiological impediment. This is a naive assumption. The conventional medical examination is designed to screen for common and conventional disabilities and diseases. A thoroughly exhaustive medical study can never be done for any case since it would be endless. Furthermore, medical science has not given us techniques for detecting many types of biological deficiency that may be due to subtle chemical and enzymatic defects, constitutional peculiarities, and delicate imbalances in the body physiology or neural organization that may be handicaps without constituting diseases. Also there is the possibility that long disuse of a function may lead to an inability to exercise that function even in the absence of a medical defect. For all of these reasons, a judgment about capacity for development and growth must inevitably be a complex judgment and can never be based merely on the results of a medical examination or on the results of a psychological test. It has to involve all of these parameters—medical examination, psychological test, developmental history, and empirical observation of the child; in many cases frank confession of uncertainty will prove to be more helpful than hasty consolidation of conviction.

It is a pleasure for the authors to acknowledge the many invaluable suggestions from their colleagues. In addition to those already mentioned, we especially thank Mary Bernard, Herbert G. Birch, Frances A. Connor, Deborah Edel, Abraham Haklay, Sharon Hobbs, Sam J. Korn, and James Posner.

Joseph Wortis

Introduction

This manual is designed to be used as a guide in evaluating the educational potential of preschool children by teachers, psychologists, nurses, and others who work with young children in or around the educational situation. It is a supplement to the text by Else Haeussermann *(Developmental Potential of Preschool Children*. New York, Grune & Stratton, Inc., 1958), and no attempt has been made to duplicate the invaluable material found in the original text. The intention here has been to simplify the material for expeditious administration, and to expand the material so it would apply equally well to children without physical handicaps. It will be helpful to consult the Haeussermann text for enriched appreciation of the child's responses. When evaluating handicapped children—those with marked physical, motor, intellectual or emotional deviations—the use of the text is essential. To facilitate complementary use of the Haeussermann text, items in this manual show references to it; where no such cross-reference is indicated, the item did not appear in the original text, and it is now presented for the first time.

It is the intent of this manual to provide to child development workers, especially teachers of preschool children, a readily available easily mastered systematic method for determining the psychoeducational standing of each child in a preschool program. With this kind of psychoeducational assessment at hand, the teacher-evaluator can set her immediate training goals and develop the appropriate curriculum for the individual child. Furthermore, by design, some main test items are followed by a graded series of teaching probes to provide for a fine adjustment of the teaching level. In fact, the teacher is teaching the child with a classroom sample of educational material as she evaluates him. By assessing his response to these teaching probes she identifies his current educational competence and the style in which to approach him most effectively.

Nature and Purpose of an Educational Evaluation

The educational evaluation is a structured testing and educational procedure designed to assess the child's present functions and level of achievement in a variety of areas. It provides an opportunity to watch the child learn under standardized conditions and to explore his capacity to master new learning. It seeks to discover the obstacles which may be present in the form of specific deficits. Subtle impairments which are not easily discernible may warrant further investigation by a specialist. The evaluation provides a curriculum guide for the teacher; the educational profile of the

1

child is a basis for planning the educational program, based on the systematic and detailed information revealed about the child. By providing an individualized diagnostic teaching program early in the child's educational career, it may be possible to avoid establishing or compounding habits which handicap his learning. The child may be trained to circumvent specific disabilities and, in some cases, to improve his functioning in areas in which he has deficits.

This is an educational evaluation, not a standardized test. It supplements the information gained by means of standardized tests. The focus here is on careful observation and response, rather than score; functional analysis and achievement capacity, rather than failure. Unlike most standardized tests, the exercises in this manual probe the child's competence in the area being investigated. The emphasis is on a simultaneous, systematic observation of the child's total behavior while responding, without limiting attention to the correctness or incorrectness of responses. The interest here is in exploring how the child has arrived at a solution and whether he has had to detour impaired areas of functioning in order to respond successfully, and not in determining how his performance score compares to that of other children.

The educational evaluation provides no norms. Standardized tests are available when it is necessary, for some special reason, to measure the child against the performance of the majority of children his age. In the educational situation, norms are easily misinterpreted and may be put to ill use. In many cases, norms become a guide to labeling children, classifying them for "homogeneous grouping," and thus limiting the instruction available to them. This evaluation is to be used solely to provide a basis for individualized diagnostic and prescriptive teaching.

The educator or observer, in addition to noting whether the child responds appropriately (or correctly) to each task set before him, simultaneously observes the way in which the child organizes his resources to meet the requirements of the situation. During the course of the interview the evaluator accumulates a picture of the child's style of behavior; she will observe general behaviors and skills which serve either to facilitate or impede learning. The child may be cooperative, agreeable, persistent, with a long attention span; he may be patient, responsive, confident; all of these general behaviors tend to facilitate learning. He may be restless, inattentive, impulsive, easily distracted; these general behaviors tend to handicap learning. The pattern of these behaviors may be observed in the child's approach to every situation.

It must be kept in mind that an educational evaluation, or even a standardized test, reveals little that an observant and experienced teacher does not eventually find out for herself in daily contact with the child. The structured evaluation makes it possible to assess the child more quickly and thoroughly in order to expedite educational planning, or to probe those areas which the teacher, even after extended classroom observation, still finds puzzling.

Area of Functioning and Test Items

Specific learning skills in five areas of functioning are investigated by the 41 test Items. For effective learning, the child must acquire skills in the areas of (1) physical functioning and sensory status, (2) perceptual functioning, (3) competence in learning for short-term retention, (4) language competence, and (5) cognitive functioning. The teacher may investigate the child's competence in each of these areas through the test Items which tap specific skills.

Within each functional area, designated as a *Section*, the Main Items are generally arranged in a sequence of increasing intellectual demand, culminating in a preschool level of mastery. Thus, it is expected that the child entering school will be able to deal successfully with the most difficult Items in this manual. The introduction to each section describes the area and skills being investigated in that section.

They are presented so that the examiner may know what to look for, and so that he may anticipate how their presence or absence will affect the child's performance in and out of school. The performance on all Items forms the basis for an individualized diagnosis and teaching plan for the child in the preschool program. Should puzzling questions about appropriate class or school placement persist, it may be necessary to consult a psychiatrist, neurologist, ophthalmologist, audiologist, or other specialist for further evaluation. Pending the outcome of such consultation, it is reassuring that the conscientious teacher, by using this evaluation, may have a basis for a teaching plan which can, in the interim, improve the level of the child's functioning and alter his learning skills. It is not necessary to defer teaching the child pending the outcome of the consultation; individualized diagnostic teaching is an essential part of the child's treatment, and the teacher's continued observations are invaluable in assisting the consultant in making his diagnosis.

It is possible, with the systematic sampling of skills provided by the range of Items, to sample intact skills, and also to explore the nature and extent of impairment when it is present.

Consistencies and inconsistencies across the range of tasks should be clear from the profile of the child's functioning. For example, the child may handle color only at the concrete level, while he can deal with shapes at the verbal level. Individual differences are thus clearly revealed with this instrument.

Main Items

The Main Items in each section are in ascending order of difficulty, culminating in mastery of that functional area at the level appropriate for entrance to first grade. The sequence of Items is designed to parallel growth demands made on the child during his preschool years, in those skills which he will need at school. Within each section it is recommended that the Items be presented to older children in descending order and that the youngest children be given the Items in ascending order. This serial ordering also enables the evaluator to use the successive Items as measures of the child's progress after a period of training when he is reevaluated by these tests. The examiner has the option of exploring all areas of the child's functioning (administering all Main Items in all sections), or investigating only those areas that are puzzling to him (administering Main Items in selected sections). In either case, the educational diagnosis deriving from the child's performance should at the same time serve as an individualized curriculum guide or teaching plan for that child.

Titles of the Items clearly refer to the skills tapped by each item. An attempt has been made to isolate functions completely. For example, Main Item 2 investigates visual acuity, requiring the child to select from the table in front of him a toy which matches a picture ten feet away, in order to determine whether the child sees adequately. It is clear that in order to select the appropriate toy, the child must not only see the picture, but he must also understand the verbal instructions, and he must be capable of accepting a picture as a symbolic representation of a concrete toy. He must also be attentive and cooperative. If the child does not select the appropriate toy, the sensitivity and skill of the examiner will be required to determine whether indeed the child has a visual problem, or whether some other factor intrudes. The test is at best only a neutral tool; the evaluator or examiner must use it to best advantage.

As the child performs successfully on the first Main Item in the section being administered, the examiner then presents each of the succeeding Items in order. When the child is not able to meet the demands of the task to demonstrate the skill tapped by that Item, Probes are provided.

Probes

Probes, administered when the child has difficulty performing the Main Item, permit both lateral and downward modification of the requirements of the Main Item. The Probes investigate the amount and kind of assistance the child needs in order to perform, and they explore the effect of training on his learning the skill investigated. We are not satisfied to say, "The child does not know colors." The good teacher is cautious about saying the child knows "nothing." She analyzes his performance very carefully to discover his present level, which is rarely nothing.

For example, if the child cannot name colors, he may be asked to select blocks of different colors as the examiner names the colors. If he cannot do this, the task may be simplified by presenting a limited choice (only three instead of six) of widely disparate colors (for greater contrast). If he can do this, he may be presented with the six once more, to explore whether he benefited immediately from this very brief bit of training. If he could not select the three, the task may be further simplified by having him match the three blocks with three similarly colored blocks (thus eliminating the need for knowing color names). If this fails, the task may be made even more concrete and more meaningful for the child by providing colored doll's socks to be matched instead of the blocks. This description differs from the actual test Item (Main Item 7) in order to present a concrete portrayal of the rationale for the Probes. The teacher will, from the point at which the child performs successfully, train him by moving through the levels suggested by the Probes. In some cases, the Probes clearly indicate what approach or assistance the child needs in order to achieve. Modifications generally move from abstract to concrete demands; frequently the number of choices available to the child is reduced; often he is offered additional cues for learning, such as tactile and kinesthetic stimuli; and on occasion verbal requests are eliminated.

Who May Be Evaluated

This evaluation is intended to be used with any child who is functioning at a preschool level, and for whom an educational plan is being formulated, be it a preschool program or the possibility of admission to the first grade. It will be particularly helpful for use with children who are difficult to test with standard tests. Such children present a variety of problems: Some children have difficulty relating to the examiner. Some relate to the examiner, but have motor handicaps or speech difficulties. Some children, because of immaturity, retardation, or a deprived or foreign-speaking background, have difficulty in understanding the instructions and in formulating adequate responses. For specific instructions on how to evaluate children with these handicaps, for the fearful, shy child, or for the nonspeaking child, the Haeussermann text is replete with suggestions.

When to Administer the Evaluation

Time of administration will vary with the circumstances. The evaluation may be administered all in one session or it may be spread out over several meetings. If the child's teacher uses it, she may gain most of the information in the classroom during the course of normal instruction, and probe only the puzzling areas in an individual "structured" interview.

One note of caution is in order: An interview should be arranged for the time of day when the child is usually most alert; it is important to avoid scheduling the evaluation at the child's usual nap time.

Preparation for Testing

Thoughtful preparation of the room and the materials will facilitate smooth and rapid conduct of the interview. The child's developmental data and history should be available, either from interviews with the parent or from a clinical study. The examiner should see these records before seeing the child, even though the focus of the evaluation is on what the child does now. Not only will this help the evaluator to understand the child, but it will help prepare the evaluator for counseling the parent in specific areas of child management which are indicated by the evaluation. The educator and parent can then work together to plan for conjoint training of the child.

The test area, during the specially scheduled session, should be as free as possible of distractions. The table should be completely free of materials, except those being used at the moment in any test item. Materials to be used in testing should be readily accessible, and at arm's length, but out of the child's reach and in such a spot that he will not look at them or reach for them. In most cases, it will be easier to administer the items if the examiner sits at the table directly opposite the child. The child should not face a window directly, since that may be a source of distraction as well as glare. If the child has physical handicaps, has difficulty with balance in sitting, or is so active that he requires restrictions for testing, helpful suggestions will be found in the Haeussermann text (pp. 41-42). Some children are most at ease on the floor; if the examiner is sufficiently agile to be able to present the test Items on the floor, this should be done.

Sample forms on which the examiner may record the evaluation and observations are found in Appendix I. It is important to use the manual and the recording form as unobtrusively as possible, in order to avoid distracting the child. After some experience with the Items and materials, it will be possible for the examiner to record her observations directly after the interview, instead of doing so while the child is present. A + should be noted next to each item successfully performed, a — to indicate an inability to perform the test and a need to probe further. Additional observations of the child's behavior during testing should be noted in the column at the right for later study and analysis when the report is summarized. Space is also provided for noting suggested teaching plans that the evaluator feels would be successful for individualized instruction.

Beginning the Interview

Every moment of contact with the child is important. If this is the first time the examiner has met the child, the very first observations of the child's behavior are invaluable. The evaluator will observe whether the child is ready to accompany her alone or whether the mother must come along. If the child holds back, clings to the mother, or looks very worried, the examiner may casually invite the mother as well as the child into the room, indicating where the mother is to sit. The mother should be seated behind and to the side of the child. If the mother's presence can be dispensed with, the examiner may dismiss the mother quietly, telling her, *We will see you when we are finished.*

"A nonverbal but friendly management of the child for the first few minutes of the interview seems to be more reassuring for many children than verbal communication. It absolves the child from an obligation to speak, which is especially important if he is shy, immature or has poor speech. This kind of nonverbal management is very different from a 'silent treatment,' which would only serve to bewilder the child. Rather it is a smiling, friendly, surehanded concern with the child's comfort and should give a feeling of mutual preparation for a pleasant visit. It should help to make the child feel that he and the examiner will be able to get along with each other. If a child is quite verbal and if he is responsive in conversation, the examiner will of course respond in kind." [Haeussermann, E.: *Developmental Potential of Preschool Children*. New York: Grune & Stratton, Inc., 1958, p. 71.]

"If, after a few moments, a child who apparently was ready to remain without his mother changes his mind and decides that he wants her after all, the examiner casually complies without giving the impression that this is unusual or a big concession. If, however, a child expresses a wish to see his mother halfway through the interview, it is best either to let him go to 'tell his mother how well he is doing,' or perhaps go with him to give this reassuring information and then lead him casually but firmly back to the room." [Haeussermann, E.: *Developmental Potential of Preschool Children.* New York: Grune & Stratton, Inc., 1958, p. 72.]

Before the child is taken to the room, a warm-up toy should be placed on the table or the floor—a musical top, a large ball, a doll, a picture book. The toy gives the child time to adapt to the room, to the situation, and to leaving the parent; it gives the examiner an opportunity to make further observations.

If the warm-up toy is a ball, the examiner may observe the child's coordination when he plays with it—whether he prefers one hand or uses both; whether he throws, rolls, kicks, pushes, or bounces the ball; whether he plays alone or engages the examiner or his mother in the play; how resourceful he is in retrieving it; and how long he remains interested in his play.

If a spinning top, a doll, or a picture book is used, the observations may follow similar lines—handedness, coordination, attention span, verbal communication, social interaction. A more detailed discussion will be found on pages 75 to 78 of the Haeussermann text.

Administering the Test Items

Have the materials ready, in sequence and out of the child's view. It will help to keep the child interested if he does not have to sit at an empty table and wait idly before and between Items. Remove the materials from the table quickly after they have been used. The pace of administration must be adapted to the child; slow down or speed up the tempo to meet his needs and to elicit maximum cooperation, interest, and attention. Some children, otherwise inattentive, respond more readily when the examiner holds their arm lightly.

Observations During the Interview

Look for intact learning skills. Judge whether the child could have succeeded on the Item by accident; from his performance determine what kind of support he needs. If he failed to meet the demands of the Item or Probe, determine whether it was because of distractibility or inability to comprehend.

Look at his total behavior to determine the effectiveness of his learning style. Learning style is a complex of behaviors among which are the following:

Ability to make decisions
Flexibility
Reflectiveness
Checking out one's answers
Control of impulsivity (of quick answers)
Response to concrete elements of situation (in contrast to abstract, e.g. literal responses, gives examples)
Ability to shift from one activity or thought to another (in contrast to rigidity)
Ability to be oriented to the task at hand
Knowledge of completion (and finishing at that point, instead of spoiling a completed product by continuing to work on it)
Motivation
Interest
Ability to sustain interest without interruption (a combination of distractibility, attention span, persistence with the task, restlessness, hyperactivity)
Satisfaction with success

Ability to accept assistance (in contrast to inability to do so when frustrated)

Spontaneous, organized approach to task and environment

Curiosity, exploration, questioning

Orderliness

Anxiety (manifested by hesitancy, erasures, excessive self-correction, inability to deal with task)

Sense of humor

Cooperation

Responsiveness

It is helpful to observe the child's level of competence in self-help functions while interviewing him or in the classroom. Thus it is possible to confirm by personal observation information given by the parent. The examiner may take the child to the lavatory at the end of the interview and observe his ability to toilet himself, to wash and dry his hands, to take a drink of water, to take a cookie, and to put on his jacket or coat when ready to leave. It is helpful to watch him walk up and down a short flight of stairs. Observe whether he places both feet on each tread, or alternates his steps; observe how he uses the rail.

After the Evaluation

It is the responsibility of the evaluation to ferret out the educational implications of the child's behavior for educational curriculum guidance, and also to communicate relevant findings to the child's parents, physician, or other personnel working with the child.

The effect of handicap on performance needs investigation in every case. Obstacles which the child demonstrates during the evaluation will give clues to obstacles he will present in an educational program. For example, the child who cannot adequately lower his eyes may not be able to button and unbutton his coat; he may not be able to read and write

if the material is placed flat on the table, but will need the material placed at a slant. The child who cannot raise his eyes may not be able to see the blackboard. The child who holds the crayon in his palm (palmer grasp) rather than with his fingers (pincer grasp) will have difficulty buttoning and unbuttoning clothing, will not be able to tie shoelaces, will have poor control of a pencil or crayon, will show immaturity in his written work, will have difficulty turning a doorknob or a key, will have difficulty manipulating scissors, and may be clumsy when feeding himself.

Implications of the Evaluation

No age or grade norms are given. We feel strongly committed to the position that classification of a young child is often a deterrent to optimal development. Since the purpose of the manual is to assist the teacher who wants to promote each child's personal growth to maximal capacity, the authors have provided a systematic method for looking at the *way* a child is *functioning,* leaving the assignment of a scale score to those professionals who sometimes need to make such a judgment—the pediatrician and the psychologist. In many instances it is important for such professionals to judge the age-appropriateness of a child's behavior; it is the teacher's crucial and irreplaceable role to change the behavior of the child.

In spite of the large body of data correlating child behavior with social class and ethnic background, we feel it is more productive to look at the child's individual style and scope of responsiveness to guided demands than it is to regard him as a representative of a particular social class or ethnic group. Our attitude is an eternally optimistic one—a child can learn to think and reason and make choices; his background, be it deprived or favored, is of historical import only.

Although no age or grade norms are given, a developmental framework is suggested in several ways. First, the range of the 41 Items corresponds to psychoeducational expectations for children from three years to six years. These tests are not appropriate for the child below three years of age nor for the normal child above the age of six years. Secondly, the five main sections are presented in a broadly developmental sequence, roughly parallel to stages of psychoeducational growth.

Although classificatory labels for the variety of pathological conditions related to maldevelopment are not offered, each section indicates specific nonaccomplishments that are distress signals requiring appropriate professional consultation. Wherever possible, specific suggestions for curriculum design are offered. However, it is part of the philosophy of this approach to train the evaluator to look at and listen to the child for her best cues for program development, and to trust herself to try whatever she feels is suitable.

After ascertaining the child's pattern of functioning, the evaluator can better devise and locate the educational strategies that will prove most effective in teaching him. Much of the teaching plan and many of the strategies will be suggested very clearly by the Probes and the nature of the child's failures. The ingenious teacher will create many techniques that are effective for each child with his particular profile of skills and deficits.

Section I

Physical Functioning and Sensory Status

The overall interest in this section is to insure the child against any possible neglect of professional concern about deficient areas of sensory or motor functioning. It is not unusual for children of preschool age to respond as if they can hear and see normally when they are in fact coping with insufficient or distorted sensory input. When one considers the nature of adult expectations of children's responses, particularly of three- and four-year-old children's responses, it is understandable that poor hearing or disturbed vision may go unrecognized. Children are expected to respond in a nonspecific fashion. They jump; they smile; they reach out; they sulk—all undifferentiated responses to stimulation which in no way signify the clarity of their hearing or their vision. They may in fact not be hearing and still be responding in a childlike, exuberant fashion to the atmosphere of excitement and activity. They may have distorted visual perception and still move around in the rather unprecise, wide-based style of a young child. We need to ask the specific question of how clearly does the child react to spatial cues, how distinct is his impression of auditory cues. The items included in this Section are specifically related to such queries and are meant to either rule out or indicate the need for referral of the child to a professional specialist in vision or in hearing.

PART A
MOTOR COORDINATION AND FUNCTIONING

Imbalance and uncoordination in the young child are not infrequently overlooked as possible signs of neurological immaturity because, again, we expect a certain amount of awkwardness. Since we do not, and actually should not, expect fine motor control in the very young child, we often overlook signals of motor distress in the preschool child when he experiences difficulty in holding a pencil firmly or placing small objects in appropriate niches. It is at this time that the preschool child should be thoughtfully observed— his relative smoothness in walking through narrow spaces, climbing graded walks, taking up a crayon to carry out a requested drawing or coloring assignment. The child's preferred hand should be noted. It is toward this end that the particular tasks listed in Part A are included in this manual.

● Main Item 1
MANUAL DEXTERITY
(Haeussermann, item 38b, pp. 252-253.)

MATERIALS:
Chalk, chalkboard, paper, crayon or pencil, pegboard and pegs (see photograph of materials in Appendix II).

PROCEDURE:
● Either have the child write or scribble with chalk on a chalkboard, or have him "draw something" with pencil or crayon on paper.

● Place some pegs in a pegboard within the child's view, and then ask the child to place some pegs. The request is usually implicit in the very act of offering the child the box of pegs and pointing to the pegboard.

Comment:

Degree of the child's dexterity is evident in the ease and competence with which he handles the crayon, chalk, or pencil. Inability to maintain a useful grip on a writing implement and marked difficulty in controlling the movements of the writing are signs of poor manual dexterity. Awkwardness of grasp or delay in the emergence of an attempt to reach out or use some kind of pincer movement to pick up a small object may be signs of motor defect or immaturity. Delay in the establishment of a directed reaching or pointing response interferes with responsiveness to the environment, and should be noted.

PART B
VISUAL FUNCTIONING

The ease with which the examiner feels she can transmit information visually is going to influence her selection of specific testing materials. A child's difficulty in dealing with picture cards or object displays may be incorrectly attributed to a limited learning level or style. If visual functioning is impaired the process of learning in school is restricted. For this reason the following screening techniques are proposed. The visual skills examined by these tests relate specifically to the level of expected functioning in the preschool child.

● Main Item 2
VISUAL ACUITY
(Haeussermann, pp. 98-107.)

MATERIALS:
Choose four toy objects such as a car, doll, cup, ball, or animal (see photograph of materials in Appendix II) for which there are available matching pictures (supplied; see Appendix III).

PROCEDURE:
● Place one picture ten feet from the child, at eye level. Ask the child to name the picture. If the child does not name it correctly, place the four objects in front of the child.

● Present each picture, one at a time, at a distance of eight feet from the child at eye level and ask the child to pick the object that matches the picture.

● If the child does not succeed, repeat the procedure with the pictures again singly presented at four feet.

● Continue to decrease the distance between the child and the picture up to about one foot, until he succeeds in matching or naming the objects.

● **Main Item 2   VISUAL ACUITY (cont.)**

Comment:

This approximates a test of visual acuity and provides the teacher with an opportunity to judge whether professional review is desirable. It is important not to confuse "acuity" with "discrimination." Acuity refers to keenness of vision; it may be possible to see an object or form perfectly well, but not to be able to differentiate it from another because of an inability to recognize nuances of the differences. The latter is "discrimination" which is evaluated in other items in this manual.

● **Main Item 3**
VISUAL PURSUIT
(Haeussermann, item 33, pp. 185-188.)

MATERIAL:
Flashlight (see photograph of materials in Appendix II).

PROCEDURE:
● Stand four feet in front of and facing the child. Using a flashlight, move it in a wide sweeping movement, covering a distance of about three feet on either side of the child.
● Tell the child to watch the light move as you move it in five different directions:

1. Horizontal, at the child's level.
2. Vertical, directly in front of him.
3. Diagonal.
4. Circular.
5. In-and-out, towards and away from him.

● If the child moves his head or his body, tell him that he is to hold still and move only his eyes.
● If he persists with head movements, hold his head still and use the flashlight in the other hand.

Comment:

Our interest here is in the extent to which a child can establish and maintain contact with a spot of light with his eyes alone. For a child to make competent use of visual information from the environment, he should be able to establish and maintain contact with a light with his eyes alone, without moving his head or his body. Observe if the child moves his head in order to follow the light. If he does, instruct him to keep his head perfectly still. Then note how much intervention or support he needs to inhibit his head or body movement tendencies—do you have to hold the child's head or provide some support? Also notice if his

11

eye movements are noticeably jerky, moving in fits and starts as if he is having trouble locating and relocating the light source. All these questions relate to the child's ability in visual pursuit. If the child seems to have to move his head in order to follow the light, this adaptation should be recorded. If the child does not track the object with his eyes even with support of head or body movements, and you are certain that the child understands the instructions, there is a possibility of a disability; consultation with a vision specialist should be advised.

● **Main Item 4
DEPTH PERCEPTION, BINOCULARITY**

MATERIALS:
  Plastic drinking straw thick enough to permit the ready passage of a pointer-stick; pointer-stick such as "Pick-up-Stick" (see photograph of materials in Appendix II).

PROCEDURE:
  ● Stand facing the child, who should also be standing.
  ● Show the child how the pointer-stick can go into the straw, and tell him that you are going to give him the pointer-stick so that he can place it inside the straw. Explain further that you are going to hold the straw in different positions, very still, and the child is to place the stick inside the straw in each of the positions.
  ● Then hold the straw in the various positions, one at a time, always at the child's eye level:

  1. Horizontal.
  2. Vertical.
  3. Diagonal.
  4. Pointing toward the child.

Comment:
  Note the extent of head movement and the degree of unsteadiness of the child's hand. Note his accuracy in placing the pointer, and judge the ease or difficulty with which he manages this task. If he has difficulty, observe whether he is looking at the straw and whether certain positions of the straw present more of a problem than others. Be certain that the child understands the instructions and is trying to complete the task. A child needs to make effective use of position-in-space cues for optimum use of visual cues and to improve his knowledge and orientation with regard to objects and persons around him. It is important to refer a

● Main Item 4   DEPTH PERCEPTION, BINOCULARITY (cont.)

young child to a professional trained in this field if there is suspicion of incompetence or impairment in this kind of visual functioning.

PART C
AUDITORY FUNCTIONING

Too often the child who shows uneasiness, confusion, or resistance to teaching materials that rely heavily on listening is reflecting a hearing disability, perhaps for the first time. When the child is pressed for auditory attentiveness as well as discrimination of specific sounds and sound intensities, this incapacity may come to the fore. These tests are screening measures to aid the evaluator in ruling out this possibility.

● Main Item 5
AUDITORY ACUITY
(Haeussermann, pp. 107-119.)

MATERIALS:
Three plastic pill vials, about three-fourths inch wide and three inches long. Into one vial place three teaspoons of salt; into the second vial place two teaspoons of rice; into the third vial place about six paper clips (see photograph of materials in Appendix II).

PROCEDURE:
● Attract the child's attention to an object or toy in front of him.

● Keeping the containers from the child's view, step behind him and shake each container separately (clips first, then rice, then salt) with a pause between each. Observe the child's responsiveness (in terms of a simple change in his attention) to each of the three containers.

● Main Item 5 AUDITORY ACUITY (cont.)

Probe A
SIMPLIFY THE TASK

MATERIALS:
Same as for Main Item.

PROCEDURE:
- Explain to the child that he is to listen carefully because you are going to make a noise, and you want him to tell you where you are making the noise.
- Tell him not to look. Step behind him and tell him to show you where he thinks he heard the noise by raising his arm on the side where he heard the noise.
- Shake the loudest container first, behind and to one side of him, being careful to avoid his seeing your movements. Each side can be tried separately. Each of the three sounds should be tried several times.
- If the child succeeds, the Main Item should be tried again at a later date. If the child fails, training in attentiveness to distant sounds and different sound levels should be started.

Comment:
This exercise allows the evaluator to make a gross judgment of the child's ability to hear the differences in loudness and pitch that are a natural part of his ambience. If there is a suspicion of a hearing problem, consultation with a hearing specialist is necessary.

PART D
COMPETENCE IN USING TWO SENSE SYSTEMS

As important as visual intactness and auditory skills are when independently considered, of even greater relevance to school readiness skills is the ability of the child to use his senses together. Reading relies on the blending of visual and auditory cues, as does writing and even simple arithmetic. The presence of intersensory skills is a developmental phenomenon which the teacher should be aware of in her observations of the child's approach to tasks requiring the coordination of two or more sense systems. In the following Item such observations can be systematically noted.

● Main Item 6
USING TOUCH AND VISION TOGETHER

MATERIALS:
Formboard with three forms: triangle, square, and circle (supplied, see Appendix III).

PROCEDURE:
- Present the board to the child, and ask him to take out the pieces and place them on the table.
- Then pick up the pieces and remove them from the child's sight, explaining that you are going to put one piece at a time under the table, and the child should feel it under the table and show you which hole the piece came out of.
- Starting with the circle, say, *I have one of the pieces under the table. See if you can feel it. Don't look, just feel. Can you show me which hole it would go into?* No matter which hole the child points to, follow the same procedure for the triangle, then the square, and then repeat the procedure.

● **Main Item 6   USING TOUCH AND VISION
TOGETHER (cont.)**

**Probe A
MAKE THE TASK CONCRETE**

MATERIALS:
 Same as for Main Item.

PROCEDURE:
 ● Hold the circle under the table, and actively guide the child's hands around the form, encouraging the child verbally to feel the form and try to pick the hole it came out of. Avoid using the name of the shape.

Comment:
 It is of interest to evaluate the child's capacity to integrate stimulation from two sense modalities. Since so many of the demands made of even the youngest child involve sight, sound, touch, and movement, the preschool child should be able to relate or integrate (and, in some instances, reconcile contradictions in) sensory information. At this stage of the evaluation, note the ease and efficiency with which the child can coordinate information from two dominant sense systems. If the child is not competent at this task, it is clear that training should be introduced specifically stressing this type of coordinated use of sensory data. If the child continues to be unresponsive to requests for coordinated functioning at this level, the examiner should request further professional consultation.

Section II

Perceptual Functioning

This section focuses attention on the child's perceptual functioning—the area of his adaptive development that brings him into direct contact with specific stimulation from the outside world. We are not merely asking whether the child sees and hears well or whether he seems able to make use of sensory information; we want to know *what* the child can do with the sensory impressions he receives and the extent to which we can count on his ability to differentiate between various shapes, colors, objects, and symbols or representations of objects. In a sense then, when a child's perceptual functioning is assessed, his capacity to profit from a teacher's carefully selected curriculum is being judged. The preschool child should be receptive to requests from a teacher to make such discriminations, judgments, and choices as are described in this section. However, the nature of the demand for perceptual adaptation can vary from direct and simple to complex. For the purpose of providing for the levels of perceptual competence appropriate for the several stages within the preschool period, this section of the evaluation has been divided into two parts.

PART A
PERCEPTUAL ASSOCIATION:
ABILITY TO MATCH VISUAL SYMBOLS

Main Items 7 through 11 provide a graded series of perceptual tasks starting at the two- to three-year level and concluding at the five- to six-year level. If a child can successfully deal with the latter items, he may be considered well prepared, in terms of his perceptual functioning, for kindergarten-level training. Since the items are provided in this graded, sequential fashion, the teacher may establish her level of training at the point of maximum success. One should not regard age-inappropriate performance as pathological, but should, rather, adopt the more positive attitude that this is the child's present functioning level, with the potential for further development through training.

The Probes provide an opportunity for the evaluator to understand more fully the extent of the child's competence or difficulty with a particular item. They also provide a training technique which can be used as described or amplified and modified by the teacher for the specific purpose of maximizing the child's perceptual functioning.

● **Main Item 7**
COLOR MATCHING
(Haeussermann, item 12, p. 148.)

MATERIALS:
   Six pairs of small squares: red, yellow, blue, green, orange, and purple (patterns supplied, see Appendix III).

PROCEDURE:
   ● Display all the squares randomly.
   ● Ask the child to pick out the square that matches the one you pick up, one at a time; say, *Show me one that is the same color as this one.*

Probe A
REDUCE THE CHOICES

MATERIALS:
   Same as for Main Item, but use only four pairs of squares: red, yellow, orange, and blue.

PROCEDURE:
   ● Follow the same procedure as in the Main Item.

Comment:
   If the child succeeds with the Probe, it seems apparent that he has difficulty observing and discriminating small differences, and making choices when confronted with a large array. The teacher can plan a program for the child, providing him with experience in making choices, at first accentuating differences, and then slowly minimizing them as the child learns to discriminate.
   Additional training can be planned using more concrete material such as dolls and colored socks. Put one of a pair on one foot of the doll and suggest that the child find the matching sock to place on the doll's other foot. The teacher can extend the child's experience both with making choices and with attending to difference in the attribute of color in the surrounding environment.

18

● Main Item 8
MATCHING OF SOLID FORMS ON WHITE BACKGROUND
(Haeussermann, item 10, p. 145.)

MATERIALS:

Two sets of cards with solid symbols of a circle, triangle, and square (supplied, see Appendix III).

PROCEDURE:

● Place one set of cards on the table in front of the child, with a circle in the center position. If the child does not spontaneously look at each card, point to each in turn, saying, *Look at all of them.*

● Then hold up the circle from the reserved set for the child's inspection and say, *You have one that is just the same,* indicating the cards on the table; *Show me your card that looks like my card.*

● If the child hesitates or points to the card you are holding up, repeat, *You have one just like it. Which one is it?* If necessary, hold the sample card above each of the cards on the table in turn, saying each time, *Does this one look just the same?*

● After the child has correctly selected the circle, ask in turn for the square and the triangle in the same manner.

Probe A
MAKE THE TASK CONCRETE

MATERIALS:

Same as for Main Item.

PROCEDURE:

● Name the first card "a ball" and ask the child for "the ball" among the cards on the table. Attempt in any concrete way to encourage the child to accomplish the first match.

● Once the match is made, proceed with the Main Item without further help.

● Give a second trial for each card if the first trial is incorrect.

Probes B and C
REDUCE THE CHOICES AND MAKE THEM CONCRETE

MATERIALS:

Same as for Main Item.

PROCEDURE:

● Place the cards with the circle and the triangle about four inches apart on the table. Give the child the reserve circle card and say, *Put this ball with the other ball,* indicating simultaneously the two cards placed on the table.

● If the child succeeds, give him the reserve card with the triangle and say, *Now put the funny clown's hat* (use any name the child may have previously used for the triangle) *with the other clown's hat,* and again indicate the two choices on the table.

● If he succeeds, exchange the square for the circle. Repeat the verbal instructions, avoiding gestures except to point to the cards on the table in a general way. When referring to the square, call it anything the child may have named it earlier, or just call it "a box," "a block," or even "a square."

● If the child has been able to perform correctly so far, increase the choices to three, place the circle in the middle of the row, and repeat the instructions once more with each card, using concrete designations for the cards.

Comment:

If the child succeeded when the choices were two in number, but failed when they were increased to three, his

● Main Item 8 MATCHING OF SOLID FORMS ON WHITE BACKGROUND (cont.)

Probes B and C REDUCE THE CHOICES AND MAKE THEM CONCRETE (cont.)

performance is evaluated as an ability to perceive the like-
ness and difference of the symbols printed on the cards,
and an ability to demonstrate this, acting on verbal instructions alone. The fact that he can function with such adequacy, but only in a very simplified situation, points to the
possibility of a generalized lower level of competence in
all spheres, rather than a specific difficulty in perception or
a specific auditory or receptive language disability. This type
of task is, therefore, useful in identifying the passive child
who does not learn easily from experience.

A correct performance with three choices indicates that
the child is able to perceive the three forms visually, to
discriminate between them, and to comprehend the verbal
instructions given when the task is reduced in demand and
made more concrete verbally. If the child was finally successful, he only needed more experience and was able to
learn from that experience.

Probe D
USE TACTILE AND KINESTHETIC STIMULI

MATERIALS:
Same as for Main Item.

PROCEDURE:
● Present two cards only; if the child has had little difficulty with the circle, but difficulty with the triangle and the
square, use the latter two.

20

● Help the child to trace with his index finger the outline
of each of the forms, then offer him the triangle of the
second set and help him trace the outline on this one as well.
● If he does not spontaneously want to place the triangle
on top of the stimulus card on the table, demonstrate it for
him. Then remove the top card, reverse the position of the
two cards on the table, and invite the child to place the
triangle where it belongs.
● Use verbal instruction combined with gestures. If he
succeeds in placing the triangle correctly, repeat the exercise with the square.

Comment:
If the performance is not correct, it is clear that the child
lacks competence in the basic ability to learn to associate
simply related environmental components. This is a serious
deficit and indicates the need for further professional consultation. Is it ignorance, is it deficit, or is it vigorous resistance to environmental intervention? An affirmative answer
to any of these questions suggests a further training regime.

If the performance is correct at this last Probe level, it
indicates that with training the child can learn to relate
simple elements, if he combines tactile and kinesthetic-
haptic experience with visual experience. He needs either
additional stimulus modalities to focus his attention on the
significant attribute of the environment—in this case, form—
or he needs to have stress in his learning placed on a
modality other than vision. Further experience with simple
direct training of this kind of child will help the evaluator
distinguish between a need for multimodal stimulation to
funnel his visual energy, and the need to regard the visual
mode as a source of weak or confused signals. (Other test
Items in the Manual are helpful in arriving at a clearer
impression of the source of the difficulty with visually
presented information.)

● Main Item 8   MATCHING OF SOLID FORMS ON WHITE BACKGROUND (cont.)

Probe E
PLACE THREE-DIMENSIONAL FORMS IN FORMBOARD

MATERIALS:
   Formboard with three forms: circle, square, and triangle (supplied, see Item 6, Appendix III).

PROCEDURE:
   ● Remove the forms from their holes and place them within the child's reach, each in front of its appropriate hole.
   ● Ask the child to replace the three forms in their appropriate holes.
   ● The child should be trained at the simplest of all form-matching levels, with the board in this position, and then with the board rotated after the three blocks are removed.

Comment:
   The child should be able to replace the three blocks after the board has been rotated. Although an achievement of the lowest age level, this offers the possibility for further training. With no competence achieved at this level, it is unproductive to proceed with training in visual perception. The child is not ready for organizing even simple responses to perceptual tasks. It is recommended that a professional be consulted and that active instruction be postponed for several months.

● Main Item 9
MATCHING OF SMALL OUTLINE FORMS
(Haeussermann, item 39, p. 202.)

MATERIALS:
   Two sets of five cards each with small black outline drawings of circle, square, triangle, cross, and diamond (supplied, see Appendix III).

PROCEDURE:
   ● Place one set of cards on the table in random order; the only consideration is to avoid placing the diamond and the triangle next to each other.
   ● Present for the child's inspection the card with the cross from the reserve set. Say, *Which of your cards looks exactly like that?*
   ● If he succeeds, present in sequence the circle, the triangle, the square, and the diamond.

Comment:
   Success here demonstrates ability to discriminate visually between forms, and to match with a minimum demand for motor performance, just indicating by pointing or eye movements. If the child does not meet the demands of the task, Probes are offered to distinguish between inability to discriminate forms and confusion resulting from having to choose from a large group of stimuli.

Probe A
REDUCE THE CHOICES

MATERIALS:
   Same as for Main Item.

PROCEDURE:
   ● If the child can succeed with a few of the forms but

● **Main Item 9   MATCHING OF SMALL OUTLINE FORMS (cont.)**

Probe A   REDUCE THE CHOICES (cont.)

fails with the triangle, diamond, and perhaps the square, then remove the ones he was able to match and repeat the procedure with the difficult ones. Give a second trial with the choices reduced to two of the cards he failed earlier.

● If he succeeds with at least one of the forms failed earlier, try again, this time adding the third form of those failed earlier.

Comment:

This probe is to determine whether the child can discriminate on a simple level between the forms he previously confused.

**Probe B
USE TACTILE AND KINESTHETIC STIMULI**

MATERIALS:

Same as for Main Item.

PROCEDURE:

● If the child has failed again, possibly confusing the diamond with one of the other cards, place the cards before him on the table and help him to trace the outline with the index finger of his leading hand.

● Then give another trial and observe whether or not he can now succeed.

**Probe C
REDUCE THE CHOICES FURTHER**

MATERIALS:

Same as for Main Item.

PROCEDURE:

● If the child fails on all five cards, give trials with a reduced number of cards until you can demonstrate to your own satisfaction that he either can or cannot learn to match the forms.

● If he begins to succeed when the choices are reduced in number, increase the number slowly by one.

● Main Item 10
RECOGNITION OF CONFIGURATION OF DOTS
(Haeussermann, item 37, p. 195.)

MATERIALS:

Two sets of seven cards with small black dots (supplied, see Appendix III). Each set of cards bears configurations ranging from one to seven dots.

PROCEDURE:

● Place on the table in random order one set of seven cards, each bearing a different number of dots.

● Say, *See these nice cards? They have little dots on them.* Indicate the card with the two dots and point to each dot on this card in turn, saying, *See, here and here, two little dots.*

● Indicate the card with one dot next, point to it, and say, *This has only one dot on it, hasn't it?*

● Indicate the card with three dots and point to each dot in turn, saying, *And here is one that has this many dots on it.*

● Indicate with an inclusive gesture all of the cards on the table and say, *You have a lot of cards here, don't you? Now we are going to see if you have sharp eyes. I will show you one of my cards and then you look around until you find one that looks exactly the same. This is the one we will need. You show me. Ready?*

● Present, in order, the cards with two, one, seven, four three, six, and five dots for him to match.

● A second trial is given if the child commits one or two errors.

Comment:

Competence in matching dot configurations is required for reading readiness.

Probe A
REDUCE THE NUMBER OF CHOICES

MATERIALS:

Same as for Main Item.

PROCEDURE:

● If the child succeeds with cards like two, three, one, and six, but confused four with five and four with six, remove the cards with six and five dots, and repeat a presentation of the remaining cards. If he succeeds, add the other cards again and repeat a trial with a presentation of five, then two, then six, then four, then seven.

● If errors persist but the child is still willing to go on, remove the cards which give him no trouble, namely those with configurations of one, two, and probably three dots, and give a few trials with the higher configurations only until it becomes clear whether he can match them or not.

Comment:

His difficulty may be a combination of inadequate attention to details, or failure to recognize their significance, with immaturity in organizing his attack on a task appropriately. This may be on the basis of intellectual immaturity or it may be unwillingness to cooperate in a task which is as yet too abstract and meaningless to the child.

If the child is successful on Probe A, this indicates his ability to learn from additional experience.

Probe B
DEMONSTRATE NONVERBALLY

MATERIALS:

Same as for Main Item.

● **Main Item 10   RECOGNITION OF CONFIGURATION OF DOTS (cont.)**

Probe B   DEMONSTRATE NONVERBALLY (cont.)

PROCEDURE:

● Place only the three pairs of one, two, and three dot configurations on the table in random order.

● Guide the child's index finger in tapping the dots on each of the six cards. If he counts them, let him do so, but counting should not be suggested as a device for differentiating the cards, since this task explores his perception of designs as well as amount concepts.

● Now place one set of three cards on the table so that from the child's left to right in one row, separated by about four inches, are displayed the one, then the three, then the two dot cards.

● Place the three reserve cards on the table and demonstrate how you compare, by holding one card at a time next to those in the row until you find the one that looks exactly the same. Place it on top of its companion card. Continue until you have sorted the three cards.

● Motion toward the three piles and remove the top card of each. Spread these reserve cards out before the child and ask him to place each card with the one in the row that is the same.

● If he succeeds now, he should be given a second chance to perform in the standard presentation.

Comment:

If a child who previously seemed unable to succeed begins to function adequately in this Probe when offered a choice of three (demonstrated as described), he may have failed to comprehend the nature of the task earlier. It is also possible that an approach other than visual was helpful.

24

● **Main Item 11
MATCHING OF NUMBERS AND WORD CONFIGURATIONS**
(Haeussermann, item 40, p. 204.)

MATERIALS:

Two sets of six cards each with black manuscript printed words: *home, cat, tac, sat, 2, 4* (supplied, see Appendix III).

PROCEDURE:

● Say, *Watch what I do.* While the child watches, place on the table one set of cards in this order, starting on the child's left: *2, sat, home, tac, 4, cat.*

● Allow a few moments for him to look at the cards. Then say, *Ready?* Present the reserve card with *cat* on it, and while holding it slowly over each card going from the child's left to his right, say, *Which one looks exactly like this one?*

● Then hold the card over the center of the line of cards and wait for his reply. It may be necessary to add, *Look at all of them until you find one just like the one I am holding. There is no hurry.* If he wants to hold the card himself or have a closer look, oblige him.

● Whether he succeeds or not with this first card, go on and present the other cards in this order: *2, home, 4, sat, tac, 2, cat,* in the same manner. Remind him that he need only look at or point to the card; he need not pick it up, although he may if he wishes to.

Comment:

Failure may indicate a need for reading readiness activities. The child's response to the probes will confirm or reject this possibility.

● Main Item 11   MATCHING OF NUMBERS AND WORD CONFIGURATIONS (cont.)

Probe A
REDUCE THE CHOICES

MATERIALS:
Same as for Main Item.

PROCEDURE:
● If he succeeds with all but *cat, tac,* and *sat,* give a trial using only these cards. If he can eventually match all of these three correctly, add the card with *home* on it and give one more trial. Increase until you present a choice of six cards.

Probe B
MAKE THE TASK CONCRETE

MATERIALS:
Same as for Main Item.

PROCEDURE:
● Leave the cards with *tac* and *cat* before the child. Tell him that you can see that this card has an airplane right at the front while the other one has it at the end (*tac, cat*).
● If he agrees, give another trial to see whether he can now succeed with all of the six cards.
● If he fails, look back to his results on Item 8 for simple form discrimination.

Comment:
More maturation and more reading readiness training are needed for complex discrimination.

Probe C
MATCHING LETTER SYMBOLS

MATERIALS:
Two sets of individual cards with the following letter symbols: *p. b, d, q, m, n, h* (supplied, see Appendix III).

PROCEDURE:
● Place one set of cards on the table.
● Present the reserve card with *d* on it. Hold it to the child's left of the model set, and say, *Which one looks exactly like this one?*
● Present six more cards to be matched.

PART B
PERCEPTUAL ORGANIZATION: ORGANIZATION OF BEHAVIOR BASED ON PERCEPTUAL CUES

As in Part A, Part B is pertinent to classroom demands, but it constitutes an area of demand that is more complex because cognitive features are also involved: the ability to understand how constructions are prepared from parts of larger shapes, from sticks, and with pencil and paper. To succeed with tasks in this part of the perceptual section, the child has to adapt to both perceptual demands and the request for action—self-guided—based on perceptual and constructional competence.

The six Main Items in this section require the child to receive and organize structured visual information. Starting with the simplest demands and proceeding to the level of performance appropriate for the five- or six-year-old child, these Items allow the evaluator to observe the child's competence in actively relating his movements to a purposeful, visible goal. Instructions are given either verbally or as a model to be reproduced. Tasks are carried out through a sequence of planned movements in order to satisfy the teacher's request. Simply recognizing and choosing a form that matches another form, the essence of the earlier levels of perceptual functioning evaluated in Part A, are relevant but not sufficient for adequacy in performing these tasks. The child has to actively enter into an organizing relationship both with the material at hand and with the teacher's proposed goal. The child must keep the task in mind and understand its purpose, he has to be able to sustain his motivation to complete the task, he has to do some simple filtering and screening so that he is not distracted, and he has to provide simple self-checks on his performance so that he can make his performance come as close as possible to the requested conclusion.

● **Main Item 12**
FITTING TWO HALVES OF A CIRCLE ON REQUEST
(Haeussermann, item 17, p. 159.)

MATERIALS:
One circle cut in half (supplied, see Appendix III).

PROCEDURE:
● Place the two halves of the circle in front of the child so that the cut edges are toward the outside. Say, *Put these two pieces together to make a ball.*

Comment:
By plan or through trial and error, the child is able to compose a form from two parts, on verbal request alone. This is different from Item 15 in which this construction is demonstrated.

Probe A
FITTING TWO HALVES OF A CIRCLE WHEN DEMONSTRATED

MATERIALS:
Same as for Main Item.

PROCEDURE:
● Place the two halves next to each other on the table with the straight edges parallel to the side of the table directly in front of the child. Say, *Look what I can do. I can make a ball.*
● Push the two halves together to complete the circle. Leave them in this position for the child to study. Say, *Do you want to make a ball?* and push the two halves back in their original positions.
● If the child fails, give a second demonstration, repeating the above instructions.

● **Main Item 12   FITTING TWO HALVES OF A CIRCLE
ON REQUEST (cont.)**

**Probe B
FITTING TWO HALVES OF A PICTURE**

MATERIALS:
Picture of a cat cut in half vertically (supplied, see Appendix III).

PROCEDURE:
● Place the two halves of the cat before the child so that the cut edges are on the outside, and say, *Put these two pieces together and make a cat.* If he is successful, go to Probe C.

Comment:
If the child is successful, his previous failure was probably due to lack of experience (with this material) and some difficulty in understanding at first. The more concrete practical representation made this task easier for the child.

**Probe C
MOVING ONLY ONE PIECE OF PATTERN**

MATERIALS:
One half of the circle in the Main Item.

PROCEDURE:
● To explore the possibility that the child is unable to *imitate* the motor act required in turning the pieces, have the child imitate your turning one cardboard piece at a time.

Comment:
Failure here would raise the question of whether the child is ready for placement in a school program.

● **Main Item 13
FITTING TWO HALVES OF A SQUARE
AFTER DEMONSTRATION AND VERBAL DESCRIPTION**
(Haeussermann, item 36, p. 191.)

MATERIALS:
One square cut diagonally (supplied, see Appendix III).

PROCEDURE:
● Place the two pieces of the square next to each other on the table, both with the right angle to the child's left.
● Say, *Look what I can make.* Hold the piece on the left of the child fixed in its place flat on the table with one hand, and rotate the other triangle until the two diagonal sides meet to form a square. Bring them together and say, *See, I made a box.* (If the child understands "square" or uses this spontaneously, say "square" instead of "box.")
● Return the triangle which has been moved to its original position and say, *Your turn; now you do it.*
● Hold the triangle on the left of the child flat on the table with your hand while he manipulates the other piece. If he wishes to pick up both or one of the pieces, just say, *Fix it like I did.* But do not prevent him from picking it up.
● Give a second demonstration if the child fails, repeating the above instructions.

Comment:
In this task, the child can show his ability to construct on a simple level, after demonstration and concrete verbal description. This information is useful in teaching him.

Main Item 14
VISUAL MATCHING OF A PATTERNED ARRANGEMENT OF FORMS
(Haeussermann, item 9, p. 144.)

MATERIALS:

Four sets of solid cutouts of square, circle, and triangle (supplied, see Appendix III).

PROCEDURE:

• Place three sets of cutouts on the table in the following order: circle, triangle, square in the first row; triangle, square, circle in the second row; square, circle, triangle in the third row.

• Say, *See what I have?* After the child has looked at all the cards at his leisure, hold up for the child's inspection the circle of the reserve set and say, *See the ball? Find another and give it to me.*

• If the child points to or looks at only one circle, say, *I can see other balls, where are they?* and indicate the cards on the table.

• After the child has matched all the circles, restore the cards to their original order if they have been moved. Then holding up the square for the child's inspection, say, *Now look at this one.*

• Offer a name for it, such as "block," "box," or "window," or use a term the child may have used. They say, *Give me all like that.*

• Hold up the triangle, saying, *Look what I have.* Point to each card in the row in turn, making certain that the child looks at all the cards. If the child offers a name such as "hat," "boat," or "house," accept it silently. No other trial need be given if the child selects all the triangles.

Probe A
REDUCE THE CHOICES

MATERIALS:

Two sets of the cards from the Main Item.

PROCEDURE:

• Place one circle and one triangle on the table. Hold up the reserve triangle and say, *I can see one just like that. Can you?* Indicate the two cards before him.

• If he can select the correct card in a choice of two, add the square in such a way that the triangle lies in the center of the row of three cards. Holding up the other triangle, say, *Let's do it again. Find one like that.*

Comment:

If the child passes Probe A, the difficulty with the Main Item was probably due to inability to concentrate and respond to a complex task, not difficulty in form discrimination. If the child failed Probe A, check his responses to Item 8, Matching Solid Forms on White Background.

Probe B
SIMPLIFY THE TASK AND MAKE IT CONCRETE

MATERIALS:

Doll, two sets of the cards from the Main Item.

PROCEDURE:

• Present three cards of the Main Item, placed with the circle in the middle.

• Introduce the doll; as you ask for each card in turn, relate each to the doll. Place the circle on the doll's lap, calling it "a ball." Hold the triangle against the doll's hair, calling it "a hat." Place the square in the doll's hands, calling

● **Main Item 14   VISUAL MATCHING OF A PATTERNED ARRANGEMENT OF FORMS (cont.)**

Probe B   SIMPLIFY THE TASK AND MAKE IT CONCRETE (cont.)

it "a book." Return each choice to its former position on the table.

● Place the sample circle on the doll's lap and ask the child to give her another "ball," indicating the row in general.

● Then repeat in a similarly playful style with the triangle, by "putting a hat on the dolly," and ask for another hat for the doll.

● Repeat with the square in a similar way.

Comment:

Success is evaluated as the ability to differentiate and match the forms only when the task is made concrete and related to a doll or person. The difficulty may be in concept formation rather than in perception. The child may be unable to abstract, even on this simple level, the quality of form from the cards unless they can be made meaningful and the form is related to a familiar object within his experience.

● **Main Item 15
FITTING FOUR QUARTERS OF A CIRCLE AFTER DEMONSTRATION AND VERBAL DESCRIPTION**
(Haeussermann, item 36c, p. 193.)

MATERIALS:

One circle cut into four equal quarters (supplied, see Appendix III).

PROCEDURE:

● Present the four pieces by placing them in a straight row, with the curved line to the left and the radius parallel to the side of the table in front of the child.

● Say, *Look what I can make with these.* While the child watches, place the four pieces so that they form a solid circle and leave them in that position for about thirty seconds.

● Say, *See, now we made a ball.* Trace the outline of the circumference with your finger while the child watches. Then return the pieces to their original position, saying, *I'll bet you can make a ball, too.*

● It is permissible to give one additional demonstration.

● For a response to be correct, accuracy is not required, but the four radii should roughly face in the correct direction and the curved line must be on the outside of every piece.

**Probe A
USE TACTILE AND KINESTHETIC STIMULI**

MATERIALS:

Same as for Main Item.

PROCEDURE:

● Using pantomime and verbal communication, help the child to trace with his finger the outline of each quarter of

Probe A   USE TACTILE AND KINESTHETIC STIMULI (cont.)

the circle. They should be placed roughly in a circle, with sufficient space between each section.

● As you hold his index finger and trace the shapes with him, place special pressure to impress on him the *roundness* of the outer sides and the *squareness* of the corners where they meet in the center. Let him experience the straightness of the radii and show him how each section meets at the straight line.

● Then permit him to scramble the circle into four parts himself, without insisting on the original position used in the standard presentation.

● Encourage him to try to put them together to form a circle again.

Comment:

If the child succeeds, his initial difficulty should be evaluated as due to immaturity and inexperience, but probably not due to a specific perceptual deficit. His performance must be evaluated in the light of his overall functioning during the interview.

**Probe B
MAKE THE TASK CONCRETE**

MATERIALS:
Same as for Main Item.

PROCEDURE:
● Place the four quarters of the circle together while the child watches.

30

● With the completed round form between you and the child, smile at him and begin to sing or hum, "Happy Birthday to You," encouraging him to join you. At the end of the song, pretend to "blow out the candles on the birthday cake" and invite him to help. Avoid having the pieces blown out of the circle alignment.

● Make an elaborate pretended effort to "cut the cake" along both center lines, leaving three-quarters of the circle in place. Offer the child the piece of "birthday cake" by pretending to serve him with the fourth quarter. Pretend to take two pieces for yourself and give the child another piece, until the four quarters have been removed from the circle.

● By pantomime and with words, suggest that the game should be played once more and ask the child, to "bake the cake," giving him the four quarters in the standard placement of the material.

Comment:

If the child can succeed when he has been helped to associate the abstract material with a familiar and pleasant concept, his initial problem can be evaluated as one of difficulty in abstracting. Success on this Probe can be due to additional demonstrations. Continued work with the child in this area will reveal whether his learning pattern requires many demonstrations and is further complicated by difficulty in abstracting.

● Main Item 16
VISUALLY GUIDED HAND MOVEMENTS;
COPY DESIGN WITH A PENCIL

MATERIALS:

Three cards with one geometric form on each: square, asterisk, triangle (supplied, see Appendix III); paper and pencil.

PROCEDURE:

● Present the figures one at a time in the following order: square, asterisk, triangle. Instruct the child to take the pencil, and say, *See if you can make one like this on your paper.*

Comment:

Clear failures are evident. The child's reproductions are more similar to each other than to the model figures. Successes are clear when they are fairly accurate reproductions of the *form* of the model. The lines of the figures should be accurately oriented, although size is not crucial. The child's typical approach to tasks is sometimes quite clear when he copies these figures: He may be impulsive, careless, or over-anxious (painstaking, slow, meticulous, with many erasures).

The child entering school may be expected to be able to copy these figures adequately well.

Probe A
SIMPLIFY THE DESIGNS

MATERIALS:

Drawings of a circle, a cross, and a single diagonal line, each on a card (supplied, see Appendix III); paper and pencil.

PROCEDURE:

● Same as for Main Item.

Comment:

The circle should be completed, but need not be perfectly round. The form is not acceptable if it is oval or highly irregular in contour. The lines of the cross should clearly intersect, but the orientation of the two lines is not important. The diagonal line must have a clear slant from the vertical. Neither orientation nor size is crucial.

Probe B
USE TACTILE AND KINESTHETIC STIMULI

MATERIALS:
Same as for Probe A.

PROCEDURE:

● Present the circle card to the child and move the child's finger around the contours of the figure.
● Place tracing paper over the figure and ask the child to trace it with the pencil.
● Repeat this procedure with the second and third cards.
● Finally, present each figure again, one at a time, and repeat the original instructions.
● If the child succeeds, repeat this sequence with the geometric forms of the Main Item.

Comment:

If the child fails Probe B, then introduce training with simple lines which vary in orientation—horizontal, vertical, and oblique. Using a flashlight, or a pointer, or even head movements (rather than pencil or finger), train the child to reproduce some of the lines. Then reintroduce the geometric figures in the same way.

Success on the Probes indicates the level at which training should start. If the child does not respond to the training provided to assist him in performing this task, this inability merits further exploration by a psychologist.

● Main Item 17
CONSTRUCTION OF STICK DESIGNS FROM MODEL

MATERIALS:
Twenty wooden matchsticks with tips removed (see photograph of materials, Appendix II); cardboard shield.

PROCEDURE:
● Place the first matchstick design, a cross using two sticks, on the table without letting the child watch it being constructed. Remove the shield permitting the child to see the design.

● Place ten matchsticks on the table between the child and the model to be copied, and say, *Use these sticks and try to copy what I made.*

● If the first pattern is not reproduced accurately, tell the child to watch while the matches are placed to form the same design, and then tell him to do the same thing.

● This demonstration should be given twice if the first attempt is not successful. If, after the second demonstration, the child is still unable to copy the stick design, Probe A should be given. If the child is successful with the first pattern either initially or after one of the two demonstrations, proceed to the second pattern.

● The first trial of the second pattern, a square using four sticks, should be given without permitting the child to observe the method of construction.

● If there is difficulty, two demonstrations may be given as with the first pattern. If there is success, then go on to the third and fourth patterns.

● For the third design, a triangle using three sticks, shield the construction from the child's view until it is completed, and then ask him to reproduce it.

● The fourth design, a diamond using four sticks, should be constructed out of the child's view. Then proceed as with the third pattern.

32

Comment:

This task of constructing figures as reproductions of visually perceived models involves different skills than the preceding Item 16. First, the child must visualize the complex pattern in its broken-up elements—a process of analysis. Then he must regard the separate sticks as possible portions of a completed figure—a process of synthesis. The child is required to deal with parts separate from the whole figure and build up to the whole. One should consider the need for a professional consultation for the child if he was competent in handling this task but could not handle even the Probes of the preceding item.

Probe A
SIMPLIFY THE DESIGNS

MATERIALS:
Same as for Main Item.

PROCEDURE:
● Use each of the following stick arrangements in the order given below.

● Present them one at a time. If the child seems unable to copy the arrangement, draw his attention to how the sticks are placed. If this fails, demonstrate the placement of the sticks. If he succeeds, present the Main Item again. If he fails, proceed with training at the level of imitated constructions. It may be helpful to introduce into the training program even simpler single-stick positions for copying, such as vertical, horizontal, and diagonal positions.

● Main Item 17   CONSTRUCTION OF STICK DESIGNS FROM MODEL (cont.)

Probe B
REPRODUCTION OF SIMPLE THREE-BLOCK CONSTRUCTION

MATERIALS:
Eight small blocks (see photograph of materials, Appendix II).

PROCEDURE:
● Build a three-block bridge: the two bottom blocks should be separated, and the third block placed on top, bridging the gap.
● Leave the construction standing and ask the child to do the same thing with his blocks.

Probe C
BUILD A TOWER

MATERIALS:
Same as for Probe B.

PROCEDURE:
● Start a tower by placing one block on top of another, and by gesture or word encourage the child to continue the tower for at least two more blocks.
● If he does not try, build a six-block tower, show it to him, knock it down, and then start building another again, encouraging him to continue.

Probe D
OBSERVE UNGUIDED BLOCK PLAY

MATERIALS:
Assortment of blocks of different sizes, placed randomly near him, preferably on the floor.

PROCEDURE:
● Encourage the child by gesture to play with the blocks. Use any means, including another child, to encourage him.

Comment:
If a child over three years of age cannot approximate a tower with blocks, and cannot show evidence of either an interest or a capacity to relate blocks to each other in any simple play fashion, the child's suitability for a regular or normal school training program should be seriously questioned. Professional consultation should be arranged to discuss the child's marked immaturity in this area of functioning and the advisability of school programmed training at this stage. With the help of special individualized training, some progress should be noticeable after a six-week period. One should not hesitate to interpret lack of progress as a signal of developmental distress.

Section III

Competence in Learning for Short-Term Retention

The previous series of Items require immediate responses to the examiner's request. The Items presented in this section derive from a certain level of competence in perceptual organization, as evaluated in the previous two sections, but put an additional stress on the child. To successfully handle the tasks set before him, in this section the child must have developed some system for briefly storing stimuli and stimuli patterns for immediate retrieval. This capacity for short-term retention can vary in scope from child to child as well as from age to age, is probably responsive to training, and obviously sets a functional limit on what a child can be expected to extract from a teaching program. The variations in short-term retention are visible in the amount of material given and the complexity of the request made.

The seven Main Items in this section provide a graded series of demands, increasing in quantity as well as complexity of stimuli presented. The ascending series permits the examiner to start with Main Item 18 if the child is below four years of age, and to start with Main Item 24 and work backwards, if necessary, if the child is five years or over. Although there will be instances of children whose struggle with these tasks appears to stem from an immaturity critical enough to require professional consultation, one should expect that observed incompetence is a product in most children of undeveloped strategies for coding, storing, and retrieving such innocuous material as shapes, numbers, and dots. A teacher can make an impact in this stage of development by helping the child to focus his attention on what is essential if he is to remember symbols rather than objects.

DELAYED RECOGNITION OF LARGE SOLID FORMS
(Haeussermann, item 11, p. 146.)

MATERIALS:

Two sets of cards, with solid symbols of a circle, a square, and a triangle (supplied, see Main Item 8, Appendix III); cardboard shield.

PROCEDURE:

● Place one set of cards on the table. Permit time for leisurely inspection, making certain that the child looks at each card.

● Say, *Now we will play a new game. We will play hide and seek.* Shield the displayed cards from view with the cardboard. Hold up the reserved card with the circle, and say slowly, *Look at this one. Remember what it looks like.*

● Expose it for ten seconds counted from the moment the child focuses his eyes upon it. Remove the sample card, and remove the cardboard so that the original three cards are visible. Say, *Which one did I show?* If the child hesitates, say, *Which of these cards looks exactly like the one I showed you?*

● After the child has succeeded with the circle, ask in the same way for the triangle, and then for the square. No further trial is necessary if the child has succeeded with each symbol.

Comment:

If the child succeeds with the circle, but fails to select the square and the triangle accurately, giving either one of these two cards (but not the circle) when asked for the square, it may mean that he only compares the baseline of the symbols. This may be true even if he was able to succeed in direct matching (Item 8). When committing forms to memory, he may limit himself to noting the most striking difference between the forms, namely that between roundness and straightness or angularity.

Probe A
REDUCE THE CHOICES

MATERIALS:

Same as for Main Item.

PROCEDURE:

● Place the cards with the circle and the triangle on the table. Say to the child, *Take a good look so you can remember them.*

● Then shield the two cards and hold up the reserve card with the triangle for the child's inspection. Say, *Try hard to remember it.* Remove the card and the shield, and ask immediately which one is the same as the one you showed.

● If the child succeeds, ask for the circle next in the same way to exclude the possibility of an accidental success.

● Then remove the circle and, while the child watches, replace it on the table with the square, still exposing only two cards, the triangle and the square. After the child has regarded both cards for a while, say, *I bet you can remember them now.*

● Shield the cards from view. Hold up for the child's inspection the reserve card with the square, reminding him to take a good look so that he will know it again later. Remove the card and the shield, and immediately ask, *Which one looks like the one I just showed you?*

● If he succeeds, ask for the triangle in the same way.

Comment:

If the child now discriminates between the square and the triangle correctly, it seems clear that lack of experience accounted for his initial failure.

Main Item 18 DELAYED RECOGNITION OF LARGE SOLID FORMS (cont.)

Probe B
MAKE THE TASK CONCRETE

MATERIALS:
Same as for Main Item.

PROCEDURE:
- If the child has still failed to differentiate reliably between the square and the triangle after the reduction of difficulty in Probe A, place the three cards on the table and invite the child to name them by asking, *What do they look like?* Suggest names, such as "ball" or "apple" for the circle, "box" or "window" for the square, "boat" or "funny clown's hat" for the triangle.
- Proceed with the task as described in the Main Item.

Comment:
If he is now successful, we may conclude that the child benefited from additional and/or more concrete presentation.

Probe C
USE TACTILE AND KINESTHETIC STIMULI

MATERIALS:
Same as for Main Item.

PROCEDURE:
- Let the child trace or help him trace the outline of each card with the index finger of his leading hand. Observe whether he looks at his hand and the form closely while doing so, or whether he looks away or closes his eyes.

- When he indicates that he is ready, offer a new trial, using only the cards with the square and the triangle. After holding up the sample card for his inspection, remove it and immediately expose the cards on the table. Give a new trial using the three cards.

Comment:
Attempt to observe which sensory modality seemed most useful in helping the child recall the forms: tracing of the outline with his hand in the air, on the table, or even on the card itself; repeating to himself the verbal designation of the card in question (the concrete name, ball or apple, or the abstract label, circle); or concentrating by closing his eyes while his finger experiments with remembered motor experiences of outlines. Make note of your observations for later use in teaching the child.

If, after this additional opportunity to learn, the child has still failed, the question of his developmental readiness in this area should be considered.

● Main Item 19
DELAYED RECOGNITION OF SMALL OUTLINE FORMS

MATERIALS:

Two sets of cards with small black outline drawings of a circle, square, triangle, cross, and diamond (supplied, see Main Item 9, Appendix III); cardboard shield.

PROCEDURE:

● Tell the child to watch what you are doing. While the child watches, slowly place the five cards of one set in a row on the table. Then say, *Now we are going to play hide and seek. Ready?*

● Shield the cards from view. Hold up the reserve card with the circle, saying *Take a good look at it. Try to remember what it looks like.* If he wants to hold it, let him.

● Remove the card, count silently to five, take away the shield, and expose the set of cards. Say, *Which one was it?*

● If he succeeds in indicating the circle, present in the same manner the cross, diamond, square, circle, and triangle, in that order.

● If he fails with some cards and succeeds with others, look back to see which forms he failed when asked to match directly (Main Item 9). If he failed the same forms on that task as on this one, do not probe further. If he succeeded without error on direct matching, but made errors on this Main Item, go on to Probe A.

Probe A
REDUCE THE CHOICES

MATERIALS:

Same as for Main Item.

PROCEDURE:

● Experiment with reducing the number of choices to three forms, and slowly increase the choices one by one until it becomes clear whether his difficulty is an inability to recall or whether he becomes distracted when there are too many forms.

Comment:

If the child succeeded on Probe A, the additional experience made it possible for him to perform successfully in this area. If he failed Probe A, but passed Main Items 8 and 9, he can recognize forms, differentiate between different forms, and match similar ones. However, he may have difficulty in concentrating and remembering and needs very basic training in focusing on and learning simple series of objects, then pictures.

● Main Item 20
RECALL OF MISSING PICTURE FROM MEMORY
(Haeussermann, item 6, p. 142.)

MATERIALS:

Three pictures: spoon, shoe, comb and brush (supplied, see Appendix III); cardboard shield.

PROCEDURE:

● Place the pictures before the child, the picture of the shoe to the child's left, the spoon in the center, and the comb and brush to the right.

● Say, *Now we are going to play a new game. I want you to remember what you see.* Point to each picture in turn, saying, *Here is the picture of a shoe, here is the hair brush, here is the spoon. I am going to hide one picture, and you tell me which one I took away. Close your eyes.* Shield the pictures with the cardboard.

● Remove the picture of the shoe, placing the picture of the comb and brush to the left instead. Expose the pictures and say, *Which one did I take away?* Be careful that the removed picture is not visible on the table or on your lap.

● Give a second trial, placing the pictures so that the comb and brush are to the right of the child. Make sure the pictures do not overlap. Repeat the instructions to look at each picture, pointing to each in turn and naming them slowly. Then say, *I am going to hide one of them. Let's see if you can remember and tell me. Close your eyes.*

● Shield and remove the picture of the spoon, placing the picture of the comb and brush in the place formerly displaying the spoon. Expose the pictures and say, *Which one is gone?*

Comment:

Ability to focus on task, attend to details, hold a goal in mind, and be motivated to succeed are all ingredients of immediate learning skill. This Item involves verbal recall and sustained attention. The ability to recognize a missing symbol was observed in the previous item.

Probe A
MAKE THE TASK CONCRETE

MATERIALS:

Comb and brush, shoe, spoon (see photograph of materials, Appendix II); cardboard shield.

PROCEDURE:

● Present the concrete objects, utilizing approximately the same procedure as for the Main Item.

Comment:

If the child recalls the missing objects, he needs training in matching pictures to the concrete objects represented by them. Start with simple and familiar objects and clear, uncluttered pictures of the objects.

Probe B
SIMPLIFY THE TASK

MATERIALS:

Three small boxes or paper cups, small toy (see photograph of materials, Appendix II); cardboard shield.

PROCEDURE:

● Place the three boxes on the table in a row about two inches apart, and say, *I am going to hide the toy and then see if you can find it.* While the child is watching, hide the toy under the middle box. Shield the boxes and count aloud slowly from one to ten. Remove the shield and say, *Where is the toy?*

● Main Item 20   RECALL OF MISSING PICTURE FROM MEMORY (cont.)

Probe B   SIMPLIFY THE TASK (cont.)

● Repeat this procedure, hiding the toy under the box at the examiner's right, and finally hiding the toy under the box at the examiner's left.

Comment:

The child should succeed in two out of three choices. If in any trial the examiner has been unable to prevent two boxes from being turned over simultaneously, that trial is considered unsuccessful.

We are exploring here the child's ability to deal with stimuli that have been removed from sight. His failure may have been due to inability to concentrate or lack of attention. Nevertheless, failure requires further investigation.

● Main Item 21 REPETITION OF DIGITS

MATERIALS:
None.

PROCEDURE:
● Explain to the child that you are going to say some numbers and you would like him to repeat them exactly as you said them. Demonstrate by saying, *I will say 5–2; now you say. . . .*
● If he is correct, say, *Fine!* and then continue with the following sets of numbers, spoken at a slow rate: 8–3; 2–7; 1–4–6; 7–2–9; 6–3–8–2; 5–9–1–6. Each series is repeated once.

Comment:

Inability to repeat digits may indicate a deficit in the ability to retain auditory information; this is likely to present educational problems. However, a child may not succeed with this item because he is distractible, inattentive, or has some difficulty in articulating fast enough. The teacher should try to train the child to focus attention on auditory stimuli at some level of interest and involvement to see if such an approach improves his performance in tasks involving the retention of a series of materials presented through auditory channels. She should also note the speed of the child's verbal response to any request for an answer to check the possibility that an articulation difficulty may be forcing a delay in response which extends the required period of recall beyond the child's level of competence.

● Main Item 22
REPETITION OF WORDS, PHRASES, AND SENTENCES

MATERIALS:
  None.

PROCEDURE:
  ● Explain to the child that you are going to say something. Tell him, *Listen very carefully so that you can say exactly what I said, in exactly the same way.* Demonstrate by saying, *Hat,* and have the child repeat the word. Try to assure the child's understanding of the task requirement.
  ● Then give the following words, phrases, or sentences, one at a time, preceding each presentation with the direction, *Now listen carefully so you can say what I say, everything that I say.*

  1. Ball. Dog. Car.
  2. Nice girl (boy). Little kitty. Big ball.
  3. Jack has a blue jacket. Mary is going to school with her sister. The big dog ran after the boy.

  ● Response should be exact even though not well articulated; no words should be added, omitted, or substituted.

Comment:
  An increase in syntax complexity is provided in the steps from 1 to 3. If the child fails on the third but succeeds with the second series, then one can assume that he has difficulty with complex sentences and syntactic rules. He therefore needs a training program geared to his level of language development for comprehension, but aimed toward fuller use of sentences that are more complex as an overall training goal.

● Main Item 23
REPETITION OF SPACED SOUNDS

MATERIALS:
  None.

PROCEDURE:
  ● Say to the child, *Listen to my claps to see if you can clap the same claps as I do.* In a rhythmic fashion, clap hands at the rate of about two per second. Follow the sequence listed, waiting for the child's response after each demonstration.

  1. One clap.
  2. Two claps.
  3. One clap–pause–two claps.
  4. One clap–pause–one clap.
  5. Two claps–pause–two claps.

Comment:
  By the time he enters the first grade, the child needs to handle with some degree of competence sound sequences in his environment. He must be able to: hear the sounds, place them in the order in which they were presented, retain them for a short period of time, and reproduce them. The accurate perception of the spacing and rhythm of the sequence is a most sophisticated level and therefore is not expected at the youngest ages. But the attempt to cope with the spaces betwen sounds by a change in beat or accent should start appearing by first grade.

● **Main Item 24**
MEMORY FOR SPACED CIRCLES

MATERIALS:
Thick red crayon, paper.

PROCEDURE:
● Say, *I will make some little red balls on this paper.* As a demonstration, make three small circles with the red crayon.
● Say, *Now I will take away the paper. See if you can make the same little red balls the same way on your paper.*
● Follow the sequence listed, waiting for the child's response after each demonstration. These are visual approximations of the sequence in Item 23.

    1. o
    2. oo
    3. o oo
    4. o o
    5. oo o

Probe A
SIMPLIFY THE TASK

MATERIALS:
Same as for Main Item.

PROCEDURE:
● Leave the demonstration circles out on the table and ask the child to copy them.

Comment:
As in the Main Item, our major concern is to observe the spacing and distribution of the visual stimuli. The school-age child should show an attempt to draw some circles closer and some wider apart.

Probe B
MAKE THE TASK CONCRETE

MATERIALS:
Six pennies or toy cars or dolls (see photograph of materials, Appendix II).

PROCEDURE:
● Arrange three pennies or toys in a sequence and ask the child to copy the sequence with the remaining three.

Section IV

Language Competence

This section is divided into two parts: Part A, Receptive Language and Part B, Expressive Language. Although it is quite evident that the separation is an artificial one in the sense that in actual practice both understanding and expression are interrelated, for the purpose of a developmental evaluation it is helpful to identify the child's instructional needs by studying first his level of comprehension and then his expressive style and skills.

**PART A
RECEPTIVE LANGUAGE**

The major concern in this part is the child's ability to respond to language as a meaningful signal for some kind of organized response, verbal or nonverbal, simple or complex. The stages of development tapped in Main Items 25 to 33 represent a progressive capacity to deal with abstract language. In this section evaluation of the child under four years of age should begin with the first Main Items and should not be expected to reach the last Main Item. On the other hand, preparation for grade-school work requires the kind of competence involved in successfully dealing with the last Main Items. Therefore, evaluation of a five- or six-year-old child should begin with the last Main Item and the examiner should, if necessary, work backwards to assess the level of current achievement and to establish a teaching basis.

● Main Item 25
IDENTIFICATION OF PICTURES OF FAMILIAR OBJECTS WHEN NAMED
(Haeussermann, item 4, p. 140.)

MATERIALS:

Three pictures: spoon, shoe, comb and brush (supplied, see Main Item 20, Appendix III).

PROCEDURE:

● Place the three pictures in front of the child in the following order from left to right: brush and comb, spoon, shoe.

● Tell the child to look at the pictures. Ask him to give you the spoon, then the comb and brush, then the shoe. Replace the pictures in their original position after each response if the child has removed or changed them.

● If the child has difficulty, one suggested training approach might be to place such concrete objects as a shoe, spoon, comb, brush, and cup on the table, starting with the shoe on the child's left. Leave six to eight inches of space between objects.

● Say, *Look at . . . , Give me . . . , Show me . . . ,* requesting each of the objects in the following order: spoon, comb, brush, shoe, cup. Replace objects in their original order after each response.

Comment:

This Item tells us whether the child can name the object while accepting the symbol in its place.

● Main Item 26
RECOGNITION OF PICTURES OF OBJECTS WHEN DESCRIBED IN TERMS OF USE
(Haeussermann, item 5, p. 144.)

MATERIALS:

Three pictures: spoon, shoe, comb and brush (supplied, see Main Items 20 and 25, Appendix III).

PROCEDURE:

● Place the pictures on the table and say, *Listen carefully. Show me the picture of the thing we can use to eat our cereal.* If the child responds successfully, continue.

● *Which thing does mother need to fix your hair?*

● *Can you find something that goes on your foot?*

● If the child names the object without pointing to it, repeat, *Show me.* Carefully avoid naming any of the objects or pictures yourself, but nod in a friendly manner if the child names it. Indicate by your manner that you expect him to *show* you the picture under consideration.

Comment:

If the child fails this Item, he may have difficulty in dealing with pictures, but understands a functional description of the objects around him. Or, he may understand the names of objects, but does not understand when they are described in terms of their functions.

Probe A
MAKE THE TASK CONCRETE
(Haeussermann, item 5, p. 141.)

MATERIALS:

Spoon, cup, comb and brush, shoe (see photograph of materials, Appendix II).

● Main Item 26   RECOGNITION OF PICTURES OF OBJECTS WHEN DESCRIBED IN TERMS OF USE (cont.)

Probe A   MAKE THE TASK CONCRETE (cont.)

PROCEDURE:
- Place the objects in the order given above. Ask, *Which one does mother (mommy) use to fix your hair? Which one do we eat with? Which one goes on your foot? Which one can we use to drink our milk?*
- Replace objects in their original order after each response.

Probe B
REDUCE THE CHOICES

MATERIALS:
Same as for Probe A.

PROCEDURE:
- Reducing the choices to two (spoon and shoe) place only these objects on the table. Ask for each in turn by describing it as in the Probe A presentation.
- If the child succeeds, remove the spoon and the shoe, and place the remaining objects on the table, presenting them again as in Probe A. If the child is successful, then place all of the objects on the table, and present them once more.

Comment:
If the child is successful in Probe B, his difficulty in passing the Main Item was probably due to an inability to concentrate or to attend to the task and select from a wide array of stimuli.

Probe C
FOCUS THE CHILD'S ATTENTION

MATERIALS:
Same as for Probe A.

PROCEDURE:
- Place all the objects on the table. Indicating each object in turn, ask the same question (e.g., *Is this the thing we eat with?*) and continue until each object has been asked for by a description of its use, while pointing to each object in turn.

Comment:
If the child is unable to use objects meaningfully, he may be very shy and inhibited and may need encouragement to play and express himself. If that is not the case, it is important that the child be evaluated by a psychologist.

If the child is able to play and use objects meaningfully but is unable to respond to verbal commands, the possibility of a hearing problem should be investigated.

● **Main Item 27**
RECOGNITION OF DESCRIBED ACTION IN PICTURES
(Haeussermann, item 7, p. 143.)

MATERIALS:
   Two pictures of children: sleeping in beds and eating at a table (supplied, see Appendix III).

PROCEDURE:
   ● Present both pictures, making sure that the child has time for leisurely perusal and looks at each in turn. Do not describe the pictures; just say, *Look at these nice pictures.*
   ● Ask the child to point to the proper picture; *Where are the children sleeping in their beds?*
   ● Then say, *Show me where the children are eating their dinner.*

Comment:
   If the child failed this Item but passed Items 25 and 26, his failure here was probably due to lack of understanding and difficulty with complex pictures. Training in language and comprehension of more complex pictures (e.g., involving interpretation of action) is necessary.

● **Main Item 28**
RECOGNITION OF "NIGHT" AND "DAY" WHEN NAMED IN PICTURES
(Haeussermann, item 8, p. 143.)

MATERIALS:
   Two pictures of children: sleeping in beds and eating at a table (supplied, see Main Item 27, Appendix III).

PROCEDURE:
   ● Say, *Look at these two pictures. See what the children are doing here and here?* In turn, point to each picture and make sure the child looks at each of them. Accept any comment with friendly silence.
   ● Then ask, *In which picture is it nighttime?*
   ● If the child selects correctly, rearrange the pictures and say, *Show me the picture with daytime.*

Comment:
   If the child fails this Item, try to teach by asking simple questions about day and night: what he does in the day and in the night, what he wears, etc.

Main Item 29
RECOGNITION OF SIZE DIFFERENCES IN CIRCLES
(Haeussermann, item 18, p. 160.)

MATERIALS:

Two cards, one with a small, and one with a large black outline circle drawn on it (supplied, see Appendix III; use only smallest and largest circles).

PROCEDURE:

- Place the cards on the table before the child. Say, *Look at the two round balls. See this one and that one?* After the child has studied both circles, say, *Show me the big ball. Which one is the big one?*
- The child may look at it steadily, point to it, or lift it from the table. After he has succeeded, replace it as before and say, *Can you look at the tiny little ball? Where is it?*
- Rearrange the cards on the table, and present one more trial for *big* and *little*.

Probe A
MAKE THE TASK CONCRETE
(Haeussermann, item 3, p. 140.)

MATERIALS:

Two teaspoons, one small doll's spoon (see photograph of materials, Appendix II).

PROCEDURE:

- Place the three spoons parallel to each other, horizontally to the side of table nearest the child, with the doll spoon in the middle; leave at least two inches between spoons.
- Pointing to each of the spoons in turn, say: *See the spoons? Look at this one, and that one, and that one. Show me the tiny little spoon.*

- When the child has responded, then ask for a big spoon.
- Replace all spoons in their original order after each response.
- Holding out your hand, say, *I will put them away. Give me all the big spoons, please.*

Comment:

If the child is successful with this Probe, but failed Main Item 29, he has difficulty in recognizing size although he can differentiate between sizes when presented with concrete objects. He needs more training in recognition of size differences.

Probe B
USE FAMILIAR OBJECTS
(Haeussermann, item 3, p. 140.)

MATERIALS:

Two large spoons (tablespoons) and two small spoons (teaspoons), all silver or white metal color (see photograph of materials, Appendix II).

PROCEDURE:

- Place the four spoons parallel to each other and parallel to the side of the table nearest the child, with the small spoons in the middle; leave at least two inches between spoons.
- Pointing to each of the spoons in turn, say, *See the spoons, look at this one and that one. Show me the little spoons.*
- Then ask for the big spoons. Holding out your hand, say, *Give me all the big spoons, please.*
- Replace all spoons in their original order after each response.

● **Main Item 29   RECOGNITION OF SIZE DIFFERENCES IN CIRCLES** (cont.)

Probe B   USE FAMILIAR OBJECTS (cont.)

Comment:

   If he fails, the child needs to be taught concepts of big and little.

● **Main Item 30
IDENTIFICATION OF COLORS WHEN NAMED**
(Haeussermann, item 13, p. 150.)

MATERIALS:

   Six pairs of small squares: red, yellow, blue, green, orange, and purple (supplied, see Main Item 7, Appendix III).

PROCEDURE:

   ● Place before the child one red and one yellow card. Say, *See these cards? Now we are going to play a game.* Then say, *Which one is red?* If further help is needed, say, *Show me (give me, look at) the red card.*
   ● If he succeeds, ask for the yellow card in the same way. After the first two colors have been identified by name, no further practice is given.
   ● Add the rest of the cards, placing them before the child so that orange is between yellow and red, and purple between green and blue. Place the whole row at the distance most suitable for the child. Say, *Now show me (give me, look at) the blue one.* In turn, ask for green, red, purple, blue, yellow, and orange.

Comment:

   Observe how the child goes about his task: whether he needs to let your verbal directions sink in for a while before responding, whether he guesses wildly, whether he tries very carefully to compare some colors (such as blue and purple, orange and yellow, blue and green). Note if he names some colors himself. Purple and blue are frequently confused even after the age of four. If a child uses designations such as "like an apple" for red, "sky" for blue, note this.

● Main Item 30   IDENTIFICATION OF COLORS WHEN NAMED (cont.)

Probe A
REDUCE THE CHOICES

MATERIALS:
Same as for Main Item.

PROCEDURE:
● Lower the demand by presenting only two or three contrasting colors at any one trial, such as red–blue–yellow, or green–orange–purple, placing them in that order.

Comment:
If the child can find the correct card as it is named for him in a choice of three under favorable contrast conditions, he can associate the correct name with the corresponding color. His difficulty with the Main Item may be in perceptual differentiation, or in the lack of appropriate color names.

Probe B
COLOR MATCHING

MATERIALS:
Same as for Main Item.

PROCEDURE:
If it has not already been done, administer Main Item 7.

Comment:
This Probe attempts to isolate the child's source of difficulty to determine whether he fails to perceive the *colors* or whether he fails to associate their *labels*. The former is a primitive perceptual skill; the latter is a language skill.

● Main Item 31
OBEYING SIMPLE COMMANDS
(Haeussermann, item 30, p. 178.)

MATERIALS:
Pencil, book, toy car (see photograph of materials, Appendix II).

PROCEDURE:
● Explain to the child that you are going to ask him to do certain things for you. Say, *Listen very carefully and try to remember exactly what I ask you to do, and then do just what I ask you!*
● Give the following directions in sequence:

1. *Give me the car, please.*
2. *Please put the pencil on the book.*
3. *Please, close the door, put the book on the chair, and give me the pencil.*

Probe A
USE FAMILIAR TOY

MATERIALS:
Choose toys that are noticeably attractive to the child based on his spontaneous choice of them as play objects.

PROCEDURE:
● At first give simple directions related to the toys, such as: *Take the doll; Push the truck.*
● If these directions are followed, ask the child to relate one object to the other in a very concrete fashion, such as, *put the doll in the bed.*

- **Main Item 31   OBEYING SIMPLE COMMANDS** (cont.)

Probe A   USE FAMILIAR TOY (cont.)

Comment:

If the child does not seem to be able to follow even these simple directions related to toy objects, observe his interaction with objects and responsiveness to people. Refer him for further psychological evaluation.

- **Main Item 32**
STORY COMPREHENSION; ABILITY TO SELECT PERTINENT PICTURES
(Haeussermann, item 31, p. 179.)

MATERIALS:

"Goldilocks and the Three Bears" (story supplied, see Appendix III); picture cards: small and large bears, small and large beds, man, horse, boat, car (supplied, see Appendix III); carboard shield; box for pictures.

PROCEDURE:
- Keep the box with the pictures closed and out of the child's view.
- Say, *Now we are going to do something you will like. I am going to tell you a story. You can sit back and rest up a little and just keep your ears wide open so that you will hear all of the story. Remember, listen hard. When I am through, I am going to show you something in this box* (hold up the closed box for the child's inspection), *something that has to do with the story. I will ask you about the story, so listen hard.* Remove the box.
- Tell the story but do not point to the pictures if you are using a picture book.
- After the story is told, shield the table from view and inform the child that you are getting ready for him. Place the objects in this order from the child's left to his right: boat, small bear, large bed, man, horse, small bed, car, large bear. Before exposing the display say, *I am going to let you look at these pictures. Some of them go with the story I have just told you. Some of them don't go with it at all. They don't belong to the story. We don't want them. You pick out all the pictures that go with "Goldilocks and the Three Bears."*
- Expose the pictures. Then say, *You can put them here* (point to the box). *Remember, you are to pick out the toys that go with the story of "Goldilocks and the Three Bears." Don't take the wrong ones. We don't want them, do we?*

● **Main Item 32   STORY COMPREHENSION; ABILITY TO SELECT PERTINENT PICTURES (cont.)**

Comment:

If, at this level of simple story telling, with a relatively narrow array of objects to choose from, the child appears to be willing but unable to be selective, the teacher should initiate a guided program for establishing some simple skills in attending to a simple, concrete task, preferably related to a series of toys.

**Probe A
SIMPLIFY THE TASK**

MATERIALS:

Toys related to a simple story told by examiner.

PROCEDURE:

● Keeping a simple goal in mind, work steadily at first on the simplest single object related to the story you tell the child.

● For example, tell a simple story about a little boy who goes to the store to buy a toy car. Then say, *What did the little boy buy at the store?*

● Increase both the length of the story and the number of toy items or characters mentioned in the story and placed on display.

● Have the child tell a story and ask him to pick out the relevant items after you have repeated his story.

● **Main Item 33
RESPONDING TO NAMED SPATIAL RELATIONS**

MATERIALS:

Spatial relation picture cards (supplied, see Appendix III).

PROCEDURE:

● Place the five cards of each set in front of the child, one set at a time. Say to the child, in random order, *Show me the picture with the cat on top of the chair; next to; under; in front of; in back of . . . the chair.*

● Do not indicate to the child whether his answer is correct or incorrect, but merely proceed to the next question. Each of the five positions should be correctly identified in one of the two sets of stimuli cards.

Comment:

The language describing relationships is more difficult for the child than that which names or labels objects. The child may be able to name many objects, but fail to understand the concepts of "under," "in front of," etc. It may be necessary to teach these relationships to him.

PART B
EXPRESSIVE LANGUAGE

The two Items in Part B allow the examiner to observe the richness and the complexity of the child's thinking processes *(Haeussermann, pp. 85-89)*. Unless the child is shy or emotionally constricted and consequently unlikely to speak unless forced to (even then very briefly), a verbal response gives relevant information to the teacher. It gives an indication of the child's thinking and expression—whether he is concrete, specific, and personal, or somewhat abstract, general, reflective, and analytical. A "lesson plan" for early childhood teaching is directly provided in this manner.

● Main Item 34
USE OF WORDS TO LABEL AND DEFINE

MATERIALS:

Toy block, ball, pencil, spoon (see photograph of materials, Appendix II).

PROCEDURE:

● Say to the child, *I would like you to tell me what a block is. Tell me all about a block.*

● Listen carefully and note the aspects of the block the child spontaneously offers. Encourage him to tell you other things about the block.

● If he does not mention the name, color, shape, composition, function, or other characteristics that you feel he might notice, slowly and carefully add these, and then go over all of them: *You see, we can say a lot of things about this block. We can say you build with it; it's boxy or square or pointy; it's wooden; it's red; there's only one.*

52

● Then give the following objects: ball, pencil, spoon. Add those you feel would be of interest to the child and note the extent to which he can offer a variety of attributes of the objects.

Comment:

In Part A, the major concern of the examiner was the ability of the child to respond to language as a meaningful signal for some kind of organized response, verbal or non-verbal, simple or complex. In Part B, the examiner should attend to the features of the expressed language, the specific quality and complexity of the phrases or sentences used.

● Main Item 35
QUALITY OF SENTENCE STRUCTURE IN GUIDED SPEECH; RESPONSE TO PICTURES AND QUESTIONS

MATERIALS:

Large picture of a family scene (supplied, see Appendix III).

PROCEDURE:

● Say to the child, "Tell me all about this picture." Encourage him to talk about the picture.

● To encourage further conversation, ask the child such questions as: *How did you come here? With whom do you play? Tell me how you play. What do you like to do in the snow?*

Comment:

Observe the facility or constriction in speaking: Is there spontaneous conversation? It will guide the teacher in assessing the child if she carefully notes if there is a difference in the richness of the child's language when he speaks spontaneously to her, to his playmates, to his mother, in contrast to the quality of his language when he answers questions for evaluation. Consider such aspects of the speech as spontaneity; richness of vocabulary; complexity of sentence structure; syntax; the use of dependent and independent clauses; the use of the four major parts of speech; verbal output; the characteristic length of the sentence; balance of enumeration and description; and overall style.

Section V
Cognitive Functioning

Cognitive functions tested here are not prominent before the age of five. These comprise the ability to develop a sense of distance and objectivity, the ability to reflect and analyze, as well as the ability to filter and screen out the nonessential characteristics or attributes of a test situation. It is therefore generally not useful to administer tests for these items to children four years of age or younger. In the case of a child who displays wide variations in his abilities (i.e., immaturity in visual-motor tasks and richness in expressive vocabulary) it is useful to administer this section of test items to gain a fuller picture of the child's capacities to observe and extract information from his environment.

The capacities tapped in this section of the manual are probably most relevant to the search for a measure of the developmental readiness for academic programs as they are now set up in the first grades of public school. In order to reach a level of development in which one can deal with the perception, identification, retention, and critical use of rather complex series of visual and auditory stimuli, all of the areas of the preceding sections of the manual would have had to be mastered. In a sense, that is what one should expect of the child entering first grade. Since, in western culture, writing, reading, and spelling depend upon the processing of visually presented symbols that represent the sounds of words, which in themselves are symbolic representations of events, people, and feelings, readiness for these skills as well as for arithmetic skills requires a measure of the kind of cognitive competence represented in this section.

● Main Item 36
GRADING OF SIZES IN SMALL OUTLINE CIRCLES
(Haeussermann, item 19, p. 160.)

MATERIALS:

One set of seven cards, each bearing one black outline drawing of a circle; the diameters of the circles increase from one-half inch to two inches (supplied, see Main Item 29, Appendix III).

PROCEDURE:
- Place all seven cards on display at random.
- After the child has inspected them for a few moments, remove the cards. Then place the cards showing three smallest circles to the extreme left of the table with not more than one-fourth inch of space between cards.
- Display the other four cards at random. Say, *Which one comes next?* indicating with one hand the ungraded cards and with the other point briefly to the three graded cards with emphasis on each one from left to right.
- No further directions should be given. If a child asks for help, silently point again in sequence and with emphasis to the first, second, and third graded cards. Say, *Think.*

Probe A
DEMONSTRATE AND MAKE THE TASK CONCRETE

MATERIALS:

Same as for Main Item.

PROCEDURE:
- Spread the cards on the empty table at random, then holding up one after another, say, *Look what I have. I have a lot of circles* ("balls" is permissible). *See, this is a tiny little one* (show one-half inch circle). *And here is a big one* (show two inch circle). *And this one is a little bigger than these* (holding the one inch next to the one-half inch and three-fourths inch ones). *Watch what I do, and afterwards I will let you do it too.*
- Place the cards slowly, one by one. Let the child see you compare and judge, even exaggerating your effort a little or waiting for him to advise you on your selections, as this will provide opportunity to observe whether he understands the task.
- After all seven cards have been presented, allow enough time to study the result and the arrangement, until the child indicates that he is ready.
- Place the first three cards on the table as before. Displaying the other four cards at random on the table, be sure that the fourth card (one and one-fourth inch) does not lie directly in line with the started row. Say, *Go ahead, now it's your turn.*
- After the child has completed the task, tell him to look it over to make sure it is correct. If the child has made some errors, wait to see if he discovers this by himself and allow as many changes as he needs to or wishes to make until he indicates that he is finished.

Probe B
REDUCE THE CHOICES

MATERIALS:

Same as for Main Item.

PROCEDURE:
- Present only the one-half inch, one and one-fourth inch, and two inch cards. Place them on the table. Invite the child to look at them.
- Then scramble the cards, pick up the *smallest* circle and place it at the beginning of a row. Say, *Which one comes*

● **Main Item 36   GRADING OF SIZES IN SMALL OUTLINE CIRCLES (cont.)**

Probe B   REDUCE THE CHOICES (cont.)

next? Display the other two cards and let him see them next to each other until he makes a choice. If he wishes to make any changes, let him do so until he indicates that he is satisfied.

● If he then should express a wish to do the whole set over again, it is permissible to let him.

Comment:

If the child fails with three circles, but passed Main Item 29 (Recognition of Size Differences in Circles), this task is probably too abstract and Probe C should be tried.

Probe C
GRADING TO A CONCRETE STANDARD (TOYS)

MATERIALS:
Three cards: one, two, and three inches square, respectively; and three pictures of bears: Papa Bear, Mama Bear, and Baby Bear (supplied, see Appendix III).

PROCEDURE:
● Place the pictures of the three bears on the table starting at the child's left, describing them for the child, saying, *Here is the Daddy Bear, here is the Mommy Bear, and here is the Baby Bear. Daddy Bear is the biggest, Mommy Bear is the next biggest, and Baby Bear is the littlest.*

● Then place the three square cards to the child's right, saying, *Now here are three cards which we will place so: One card is the biggest, one card is the next biggest, and one card is the littlest.* Do not arrange the cards to match the pictures in size order.

● Then say, *Each bear has his own card. Put the biggest card next to the Daddy Bear, the next biggest near the Mommy Bear, and the littlest next to the Baby Bear.*

Comment:

If the child fails, refer back to Main Item 29 (Recognition of Size Differences in Circles), to see if the child understands the terms "big" and "little." If Main Item 29 was passed, the child is able to differentiate between "big" and "little" and should be able to match at least the largest and smallest cards with the Papa Bear and Baby Bear, but he needs more training to relate to more than two sizes. There is also the possibility that the cards may be too abstract for him. Probe A of Main Item 29 explores whether he can perform successfully when the task is more concrete.

Main Item 37
AMOUNT CONCEPT
(Haeussermann, item 25, p. 169.)

MATERIALS:

Ten pennies of the same size and color (see photograph of materials, Appendix II).

PROCEDURE:

• Place the pennies in a row. Ask the child to give you two pennies, then three, then five, then four, then six, as long as he can arrive at correct answers.

Probe A
GIVE AN ADDITIONAL TRIAL

MATERIALS:

Same as for Main Item.

PROCEDURE:

• This time say, *I want one penny, just one.* Then say, *Give me two pennies.*
• If he is successful, go back to the Main Item.

Comment:

After this additional trial if the child was successful, it would indicate that his lack of success during previous trials was due to inattention. The child who succeeds in the Probe usually makes only minor errors in the Main Item.

Main Item 38
AMOUNT RECOGNITION
(Haeussermann, item 26, p. 171.)

MATERIALS:

Thirty pennies or plastic chips of uniform color and size (see photograph of materials, Appendix II).

PROCEDURE:

• Secure the child's attention, holding the box of pennies in reserve. While he watches, place before him on his side of the table, slowly and with emphasis, making sure you are going from his left to his right, two pennies, not more than two or three inches apart. Immediately place the same amount before yourself, going from your right to your left.
• Prevent the child from picking up his pennies.
• Point to his and your rows of pennies with emphasis repeatedly. Then indicate the child and yourself with emphasis, to let him know that you have the same amount.
• Remove the rows. Wait a moment and repeat the demonstration in the same way, using four pennies for each row. Remove the pennies after the child has regarded both rows and has had a chance to compare them in this way.
• At the third demonstration, begin placing the pennies on your side of the table, using three pennies. Then wait instead of going on and observe whether the child anticipates a row for himself. If he does, place three pennies in front of him and leave the two rows exposed for about twenty to thirty seconds. Say, *Now we both have the same.*
• Place the pile or box of pennies within reach of his leading hand. Remove the six pennies in the two rows and return them to the pile. Then place four pennies slowly and with emphasis in a row in front of you, indicate the pile of pennies and invite the child to make his own row.
• If he succeeds, help him to push yours and his rows back to the pile. Praise him matter-of-factly.

• Place seven pennies before yourself and invite the child to imitate it. If he can succeed with seven, remove the pennies as before and demonstrate slowly one row of five to your right, leave a space, which should be about in the center of the table, then make a second row of five to your left. Indicate the row of ten *without* especially emphasizing the space in the middle. Invite the child to match it. Observe whether the child places ten correctly, whether he leaves a space after the first five, or whether he ignores the space but arrives at the correct amount.

• If he finds it difficult to keep track of your pennies, it is permissible to push your two rows nearer to him to facilitate matching.

• If he has succeeded with ten, remove the rows. Do not neglect to praise the child so that he understands that he is on the right track.

• Next place five in a row, have him match it, then ask him to watch what you will be doing. While he watches, remove the two pennies at the left end of *your row as seen from your position,* push them to the pile and wait for his response.

• If he follows and removes two of his, even if he takes them off anywhere else (middle, left, or right), praise him again.

• Next, with three pennies remaining in each row, secure his attention and while he watches, push four pennies more to your row to make a total of seven. Invite him to imitate.

Comment:

Often children are observed to match poorly even when they seem able to count the pennies orally. Failure may indicate that the child may not understand counting for matching. More training is needed for arithmetic readiness. He may not understand "matching."

The child may limit the matching to the first and last items in the row and disregard the items between. This would suggest that the child is functioning on a more concrete level than required for task competence. (He has overlooked the requirement for correspondence of items between the first and the last pennies.) There is a possibility that he may have difficulty with visually guided action.

Main Item 39
FINDING NUMBERS AND WORDS FROM MEMORY AFTER SHORT EXPOSURE
(Haeussermann, item 40b, p. 206.)

MATERIALS:

Two sets of six cards each with black manuscript printed words: *home, cat, tac, sat, 2, 4* (supplied, see Main Item II, Appendix III); cardboard shield.

PROCEDURE:

• Place the cards on the table and say, *And now we will play hide and seek.*

• Encourage the child to look at the cards, then shield them from view. Present the reserve card with *4* on it, hold it up for the child's inspection, and say, *Take a good look at it. Try to remember it.* Then remove the card, silently count to five, and expose cards on the table.

• Ask the child to pick out or point to the card that matches the one you held up.

• Continue to present the cards in this order: *home, sat, 4, tac, 2, cat.*

• Give three trials with any word the child fails, alternating it with a number symbol. Repeat the reminder that he need not pick up the cards and have him indicate his choices by pointing.

Comment:

If all cards are successfully identified, it is an indication that the child has adequate memory for written symbols (including simple word configurations and single digits) for the reading readiness level.

Main Item 40
MEMORY FOR DOT CONFIGURATIONS
(Haeussermann, item 37, p. 195.)

MATERIALS:

Two sets of seven cards, with small black dots (supplied, see Main Item 10, Appendix III); cardboard shield. Each set of cards bears configurations ranging from one to seven dots.

PROCEDURE:

• Place the cards of one set on the table, behind the shield. Then expose it and, pointing to each card, encourage the child to look at all of them, starting with the child's left and going to his right. Say, *Look at every one of these cards because I am going to play a new game with you.*

• Shield the cards from his view, and hold up a card from the reserve set that shows the configuration of *two.* Say, *Take a look. Try to remember what it looks like.* After he has indicated that he is ready, remove the card and at the same moment expose the cards on the table. Say, *Which one did I show you?* If necessary, repeat the direction that it is not necessary that he pick up the card; he may indicate it with his eyes or point to it.

• Continue to present the cards in this order: *one, four, two, six, three, five, three, four, seven.* Shield the cards from the child's view each time before showing the sample card. Return any card he may have removed or which may have been pushed too close to another card back to its original position. After the first card with the configuration of *two* has been presented, try to present the cards for only as long as it takes you to give the verbal directions, *Take a look. Try to remember what it looks like.* You may ask, *Ready?*

● **Main Item 41**

MATCHING AMOUNT WHEN CONFIGURATION AND COLOR ARE DIFFERENT

(Haeussermann, item 37, p. 195.)

MATERIALS:

Same as for Main Item 40, *plus* three gray cards bearing configurations of five, six and seven dots, in configurations dissimilar to those on the white cards (supplied, see Appendix III).

PROCEDURE:

● Place the cards as in Main Item 40 and say, *Now we will play one last game with these cards. This time I am going to show you one like this.* Hold up the gray card with the five dots and say, *Which one does it go with?* Allow as much time as the child needs.

● If he succeeds, ask, *How did you know?* Find out by this inquiry whether he succeeded by chance, by approximation, by counting, or by mentally reconstructing the dots.

● Present in turn the gray card with the configuration of six and of seven in the same way. If he succeeds, no further inquiry is needed.

Comment:

This exercise requires the ability to abstract the essential feature that dissimilar objects have in common. This ability is necessary for concept formation, for categorizing, and for generalizing.

Probe A
REDUCE THE CHOICES

MATERIALS:

Same as for Main Item.

PROCEDURE:

● Reduce the number of cards on the table to the three highest numbers. Give another trial with each card.

● Do not tell him to count the dots. You are trying to find out *how* he learns, and, if he finally succeeds, you are observing the pattern by which he did so.

Appendix I

Children's Evaluation Records

To demonstrate the use of this developmental evaluation, we are presenting three full records obtained from nursery-school age children. These children represent a sample of youngsters who were evaluated because they were, in some ways, puzzling to the teacher.

One can note that the patterns of responses and the quality and style of the performances differed for these three children who were approximately the same chronological age. The use of this structured evaluation permits the teacher to obtain a better understanding, in a short time, of the current educational needs of a problem child, and it provides the basis for prescriptive teaching. In addition, the developmental evaluation offers the teacher a basis for measuring the child's progress in response to the introduction of a tailored teaching program. Readiness for first-grade curriculum can be assessed, and special areas of competence or incompetence can be identified.

A plus sign (+) is noted next to each item successfully performed; a minus sign (−) indicates inability to perform the test and a need to probe further. Additional observations of the child's behavior and learning patterns are noted with the performance of each item, and suggested approaches to teaching the child are indicated in the space at the right. These reports are samples, not models, for they will always reflect the professional interests of the examiner and of the setting.

Although not equivalent to normative testing, this evaluation schedule provides the teacher with a meaningful basis for individualized educational intervention.

JOYCE C.

Chronological Age: Four years, five months.
Educational Training: Three months in nursery school.
Presenting Problem: Wants a lot of attention, wants to be a leader, "bossy," competitive.

School Report

Joyce is a pleasant-looking, red-haired, blue-eyed girl. She is well developed physically and nicely dressed. She is the only child of professional, working parents. A maid takes care of the child during the mother's absence. They travel a lot and Joyce was in Japan and Europe with her parents. In class Joyce wants a lot of attention and she wants to be a leader. When she does not get attention, often she works carelessly and easily deteriorates in work when not supervised. When the task is competitive she works very well. Joyce is accepted by other children but not much liked; she often teases them and is "bossy."

Evaluation

Physical Functioning and Sensory Status
Joyce responded well to all tasks. Her motor control and coordination were good, and her sensory abilities were adequate. She was able to integrate data using touch and vision together without difficulty.

Perceptual Functioning
Joyce's perceptual abilities were very good as tested. She was able to match even very complex patterns (dots, words, numbers), but only after the choice was reduced. A question to ask here is, does she need additional experience to learn the task of complex discrimination, or did she fail Items 10

and 11 because she was inattentive or because the task is too hard for her age?
She had only some difficulty with Items 16 and 17. She seemed to enjoy effort and wanted very much to succeed. Her pencil grasp was good. She used her right hand. She drew a star and square but failed a triangle; the square was drawn in an immature way. She passed Probe A of Main Item 16 very well. She copied the stick figures very carefully except the diamond (she achieved only the upper part and was unable to finish the lower part).

Competence in Learning for Short-Term Retention
When she was motivated and when she had the evaluator's attention, Joyce showed very good ability to concentrate and memorize. She was able to succeed at all tasks except imitating spaced sounds and circles. She imitated simple patterns but was not yet able to understand spacing.

Language Competence
Joyce was excellent in all language tasks. She responded quickly, without hesitancy, and well. Her own speech was well structured; she spontaneously used sentences. She was able to describe pictures without prodding, her description was full, and rather orderly. Her speech was clear, her vocabulary rich. She responded well to questions, with ease, and meaningfully. The only task she partially failed was Main Item 33; she confused some spatial relations and was hesitant. Joyce might enjoy more training in this area.

Cognitive Functioning
Joyce seemed stimulated by hard tasks and eager to try. She was able to grade circles after demonstration and was very careful to compare them. She worked slowly, persistently, and achieved Probe A, Item 36. She had number concepts one to six and counted carefully. When matching pennies (Item 38) she showed more immature performance

looking for first and last to match; she matched space rather than number. Joyce needs more training for arithmetic readiness.

Educational Planning

Functioning level: Academic readiness level.
Essential ingredients to be considered for setting educational prescription:

1. Interest and motivation when challenged seems better than on less demanding tasks.

2. During testing, behavior excellent; problem when personal attention was not given.
3. In general, alert and works very well; may be asked for too little effort in class. Areas for stimulation: spatial relations; arithmetic readiness.
4. Quality of achievements good, some behavior problems in class may be due to too low level, not enough intellectual and social stimulation. Slight behavioral difficulties suggest inquiry into home situation. In school, try to give her more difficult tasks; consider change of class (older group?).

Name __Joyce C.__ Sex __F__ D.O.B. _____ Age __4-5__ School __Nursery__

Date of Test _____

PSYCHOEDUCATIONAL EVALUATION
OF THE PRESCHOOL CHILD

Item No.	Name of Item or Probe	Observations and Teaching Suggestions
SECTION I. PHYSICAL FUNCTIONING AND SENSORY STATUS		
1 __+__	Manual dexterity	Well-coordinated, good motor control.
2 __+__	Visual acuity	Able, but not particularly interested in physical activities.
3 __+__	Visual pursuit	
4 __+__	Depth perception, binocularity	
5 __+__	Auditory acuity	
___	Probe A: Simplify task	
6 __+__	Using touch and vision together	
___	Probe A. Make task concrete	
SECTION II. PERCEPTUAL FUNCTIONING		
7 __+__	Color matching	
___	Probe A. Reduce choices	
8 __+__	Matching of solid forms on white background	
___	Probe A. Make task concrete	
___	Probes B and C. Reduce choices and make concrete	

Item No.	Name of Item or Probe	Observations and Teaching Suggestions
	Probe D. Tactile and kinesthetic stimuli	
	Probe E. Use of formboard	
9 +	Matching of small outline forms	
	Probe A. Reduce choices	
	Probe B. Tactile and kinesthetic stimuli	
	Probe C. Reduce choices further	
10 —	Recognition of configuration of dots	
	Attention?	*Learned to discriminate and match letters, numbers, dots, and configurations —*
+	Probe A. Reduce choices *Needs additional experience*	
	Probe B. Demonstrate	*Practice at readiness level.*
11 —	Matching of numbers and word configurations	*Needs more experience in this area.*
+	Probe A. Reduce choices *Needs additional experience*	
	Probe B. Make task concrete	
	Probe C. Match letter symbols	
12 +	Fitting two halves of a circle on request	
	Probe A. Demonstrate	
	Probe B. Fit halves of picture	
	Probe C. Move one piece	
13 +	Fitting two halves of a square after demonstration and verbal description	

Item No.	Name of Item or Probe	Observations and Teaching Suggestions
14 ✗	Visual matching of a patterned arrangement of forms	
	_____ Probe A. Reduce choices	
	_____ Probe B. Simplify and make task concrete	
15 ✗	Fitting four quarters of a circle after demonstration and verbal description	*Excellent*
	_____ Probe A. Tactile and kinesthetic stimuli	
	_____ Probe B. Make task concrete	
16 —	Visually guided hand movements; copy design with a pencil	*Some difficulty in reproducing angles.*
	Square imitative, star o.k., but failed Triangle.	
	✗ Probe A. Simplify designs	*Needs experience in copying designs — Try use of sand, crayons, etc.*
	_____ Probe B. Tactile and kinesthetic stimuli	
17 —	Construction of stick designs from model	
	Failed diamond, difficulty with lower portion.	
	✗ Probe A. Simplify designs	
	_____ Probe B. Three-block construction	
	_____ Probe C. Build a tower	
	_____ Probe D. Observe block play	

Item No.	Name of Item or Probe	Observations and Teaching Suggestions

SECTION III. COMPETENCE IN LEARNING FOR SHORT-TERM RETENTION

Item No.	Name of Item or Probe	Observations and Teaching Suggestions
18 +	Delayed recognition of large solid forms	
	Probe A. Reduce choices	
	Probe B. Make task concrete	
	Probe C. Tactile and kinesthetic stimuli	
19 +	Delayed recognition of small outline forms	
	Probe A. Reduce choices	
20 +	Recall of missing picture from memory	Good memory. Attentive in one-to-one relationship.
	Probe A. Make task concrete	
	Probe B. Simplify task	
21 +	Repetition of digits	
22 +	Repetition of words, phrases, and sentences	Reproduced simple patterns where spacing was not involved — Not responsive to spacing.
23 —	Repetition of spaced sounds Simple repetition, not with spacing	
24 —	Memory for spaced circles Simple repetition, not with spacing	
	+ Probe A. Simplify task	
	Probe B. Make task concrete	

Item No.	Name of Item or Probe	Observations and Teaching Suggestions

SECTION IV. LANGUAGE COMPETENCE

25 ✛	Identification of pictures of familiar objects when named	
26 ✛	Recognition of pictures of objects when described in terms of use	*Good vocabulary and good comprehension.*
———	Probe A. Make task concrete	*Encourage participation in story-telling.*
———	Probe B. Reduce choices	
———	Probe C. Focus child's attention	
27 ✛	Recognition of described action in pictures	
28 ✛	Recognition of "night" and "day" when named in pictures	
29 ✛	Recognition of size differences in circles	
———	Probe A. Make task concrete	
———	Probe B. Use familiar objects	
30 ✛	Identification of colors when named	
———	Probe A. Reduce choices	
———	Probe B. Color matching	
31 ✛	Obeying simple commands	
———	Probe A. Use familiar toy	

Item No.	Name of Item or Probe	Observations and Teaching Suggestions
32	+	Story comprehension; ability to select pertinent pictures	
	Probe A. Simplify task	
33	—	Responding to named spatial relations	*Some success, but confused "next to" and "in back of"*
34	+	Use of words to label and define	*Very verbal, used sentences. Descriptive*
35	+	Quality of sentence structure in guided speech; response to pictures and questions	*Meaningful responses— "I like to play with dolls — to play school."*

SECTION V. COGNITIVE FUNCTIONING

Item No.	Name of Item or Probe	Observations and Teaching Suggestions
36	—	Grading of sizes in small outline circles	*More practice on readiness level*
	+	Probe A. Demonstrate and make concrete	*More interest*
	—	Probe B. Reduce choices	*Number concepts relatively good.*
	—	Probe C. Grading to standard	*Counts with comprehension.*
37	+	Amount concept	
	—	Probe A. Additional trial	
38	—	Amount recognition	*Matched, except when spaced, then only matched first and last.*
39	—	Finding numbers and words from memory after short exposure	*Interested, tried repeatedly. Successful with numbers, not with words.*
40	—	Memory for dot configurations	*Tried by counting but could not. Discouraged. Discontinued.* *Needs more experience with concepts of space and size, and spatial relationships.*
41		Matching amount when configuration and color are different	

RICKY W.

Chronological Age: Four years, six months.
Educational Training: Three months in nursery school.
Presenting Problem: Active, aggressive child; language comprehension at times questionable.

School Report

Ricky is a black boy, well developed physically, and handsome. Reportedly his early development was normal. He is the second of four children (six-year-old girl, three-year-old boy, and two-year-old girl). There is no father at home; the family is on welfare. The father left home and is not involved. The mother is very young; she dropped out of school at age sixteen because of pregnancy. Ricky is in nursery school on a scholarship, as his aunt (mother's sister) works in the school cafeteria. Ricky is a very active and rather aggressive child. He is impulsive, often does not listen, and his comprehension at times is questionable. He communicates verbally but also uses a lot of gestures. He is well accepted by other children, although he often fights over toys, etc.

Evaluation

Physical Functioning and Sensory Status
Ricky's motor development was good, his responses were those of a well-coordinated child. He responded well to auditory and visual stimuli. He was able to integrate data from different sensory systems.

Perceptual Functioning
Ricky's ability to discriminate, match, and recognize perceptual material seemed intact. In general, he dealt with quite complex patterns when attentive. His problems seemed to be not perceptual difficulties but impulsivity and difficulty in concentrating in order to observe details. If the importance of observing details was pointed out to him and structure was provided to prevent impulsiveness, he was able to match dots, words, and numbers. Also some concretization was occasionally given (Probe B, Item 11; Probe B, Item 15). Ricky used his right hand and his pencil grasp was good. His drawings were well controlled but he executed them quickly, somewhat carelessly. He handled Probe A of Item 16 very well but not the Main Item: His star was passable but sloppy; the square and triangle were started well, but he did not finish the angles properly. In Main Item 17 with sticks he was unable to imitate the diamond and he overlooked the inclination of lines in Probe A; otherwise he performed correctly.

Competence in Learning for Short-Term Retention
At times Ricky needed additional exposure probably because of his lack of attention and concentration. He did better when the task was concretized. If attentive, he was able to repeat four digits, to repeat two-word phrases but not longer sentences. He imitated simple claps of hands or circle patterns, but not spacing (Items 23, 24).

Language Competence
Basic comprehension as checked was adequate. Some paucity of language was observed: He could match colors but confused names *purple* and *blue;* he followed two verbal commands but not three (impulsivity? distractibility? memory?). His spontaneous response to pictures was inhibited; he named hesitantly and needed prodding. Spontaneously, he spoke in sentences and he answered questions in sentences, although poorly structured and with colloquial expressions.

Cognitive Functioning

Ricky was able to do some problems on a more concrete level (Item 36, Probe C). He was able to count a little and had number concepts one to four.

Educational Planning

Functioning level: Uneven academic readiness.
Essential ingredients to be considered for setting educational prescription:

1. Sensory intactness.
2. Good motor coordination and control.
3. Good perceptual abilities.
4. Brief attention span.
5. Some limitations in language area (cultural deprivation?). Enlarge vocabulary and stimulate verbal communication. Spontaneous speech is better than on tasks.
6. He needs development of number concepts and of purposeful counting.
7. Purposeful communication and some cognitive abilities are emerging. Needs encouraging.
8. Responsiveness, but tendency to impulsivity, distractibility, disinhibition contributes to behavior difficulties in class (aggressive, fights).
9. Needs structure, and alternation of physical activities with quiet, classroom activities. Try to handle within classroom situation. If not, refer for professional advice.

Name ___Ricky W.___ Sex _M_ D.O.B. _____ Age _4-6_ School ___Nursery___

Date of Test _____

PSYCHOEDUCATIONAL EVALUATION
OF THE PRESCHOOL CHILD

Item No.	Name of Item or Probe	Observations and Teaching Suggestions

SECTION I. PHYSICAL FUNCTIONING AND SENSORY STATUS

1 +	Manual dexterity	Good coordination and motor control.
2 +	Visual acuity	Graceful movements - In general, active.
3 +	Visual pursuit	
4 +	Depth perception, binocularity	Enjoys physical activity - may be used as reward or relaxation.
5 +	Auditory acuity	
—	Probe A: Simplify task	
6 +	Using touch and vision together	
—	Probe A. Make task concrete	

SECTION II. PERCEPTUAL FUNCTIONING

7 +	Color matching	
—	Probe A. Reduce choices	
8 +	Matching of solid forms on white background	
—	Probe A. Make task concrete	
—	Probes B and C. Reduce choices and make concrete	

Item No.	Name of Item or Probe	Observations and Teaching Suggestions
	———— Probe D. Tactile and kinesthetic stimuli	
	———— Probe E. Use of formboard	
9 ✝	Matching of small outline forms	
	———— Probe A. Reduce choices	
	———— Probe B. Tactile and kinesthetic stimuli	
	———— Probe C. Reduce choices further	
10 —	Recognition of configuration of dots	*Overlooks details, impulsive, difficulty in concentrating*
	✝ Probe A. Reduce choices	*Able to learn if forced to observe details and concentrate.*
	Probe B. Demonstrate	
11 ╲	Matching of numbers and word configurations	*Needs structure, inhibition of impulsivity, and concretization of tasks.*
	⌣ Probe A. Reduce choices	
	✝ Probe B. Make task concrete	*He is alert, and discriminates well*
	———— Probe C. Match letter symbols	
12 ✝	Fitting two halves of a circle on request	
	———— Probe A. Demonstrate	
	———— Probe B. Fit halves of picture	
	———— Probe C. Move one piece	
13 ✝	Fitting two halves of a square after demonstration and verbal description	

Item No.	Name of Item or Probe	Observations and Teaching Suggestions
14 ___+___	Visual matching of a patterned arrangement of forms	
	Probe A. Reduce choices	
	Probe B. Simplify and make task concrete	
15 ___−___	Fitting four quarters of a circle after demonstration and verbal description	
___−___	Probe A. Tactile and kinesthetic stimuli	
___+___	Probe B. Make task concrete	
16 ___−___	Visually guided hand movements; copy design with a pencil	
___+___	Probe A. Simplify designs	
___−___	Probe B. Tactile and kinesthetic stimuli	
17 ___−___	Construction of stick designs from model *Could not construct diamond*	
___−___	Probe A. Simplify designs *Could not make inclined lines. Careless. Corrected after additional demonstration.*	
___+___	Probe B. Three-block construction	
___−___	Probe C. Build a tower	
___−___	Probe D. Observe block play	

Item No.	Name of Item or Probe	Observations and Teaching Suggestions

SECTION III. COMPETENCE IN LEARNING FOR SHORT-TERM RETENTION

18 ____ Delayed recognition of large solid forms

_____ /   Probe A. Reduce choices

_____ +   Probe B. Make task concrete

_____   Probe C. Tactile and kinesthetic stimuli

19 ____ Delayed recognition of small outline forms

_____ +   Probe A. Reduce choices

20 ____ Recall of missing picture from memory
Impulsive? inattentive? or language problem?

_____ +   Probe A. Make task concrete – *better concentration?*
or understands task?

_____   Probe B. Simplify task

21 ___+ Repetition of digits   *All except 4 digits, did*
4 when strongly pressed.

22 ____ Repetition of words, phrases, and sentences
Phrases of 2 words, only.

23 ____ Repetition of spaced sounds

24 ____ Memory for spaced circles

_____   Probe A. Simplify task

_____   Probe B. Make task concrete

Needs structure or supervision of listening and concentrating

78

SECTION IV. LANGUAGE COMPETENCE

25 ┼ Identification of pictures of familiar objects
when named

26 ┼ Recognition of pictures of objects when
described in terms of use

    —— Probe A. Make task concrete

    —— Probe B. Reduce choices

    —— Probe C. Focus child's attention

27 ┼ Recognition of described action in pictures

28 ┼ Recognition of "night" and "day" when named in pictures

29 ┼ Recognition of size differences in circles

    —— Probe A. Make task concrete

    —— Probe B. Use familiar objects

30 — Identification of colors when named

    — Probe A. Reduce choices

    ┼ Probe B. Color matching

31 — Obeying simple commands   2 & 3 ok
       Inattentive, impulsive

    ┼ Probe A. Use familiar toy

Handwritten note (right column): To make him listen, encourage all verbal tasks, especially response to pictures, questions.

His spontaneous speech is better; when asked, he tends to be inhibited & monosyllabic.

Item No.	Name of Item or Probe	Observations and Teaching Suggestions
32	Story comprehension; ability to select pertinent pictures	
	Does not listen	
	⎯ Probe A. Simplify task	
33	Responding to named spatial relations	
	Confused – language impoverished	
34	Use of words to label and define	
	Enumerates with prodding. Speech inhibited.	
35	Quality of sentence structure in guided speech; response to pictures and questions	
	Monosyllabic short sentences, structure poor, uses gestures, accompanies words with rolling movements + noise.	

SECTION V. COGNITIVE FUNCTIONING

Item No.	Name of Item or Probe	Observations and Teaching Suggestions
36	Grading of sizes in small outline circles	
	Inattentive, unable to grasp	
	⎯ Probe A. Demonstrate and make concrete	
	⎯ Probe B. Reduce choices	
	+ Probe C. Grading to standard	
37	Amount concept *Not 1–6, but 1–4 DK.*	*Work on development of number concept (4 + up.)*
	+ Probe A. Additional trial	
38	Amount recognition	
39	Finding numbers and words from memory after short exposure *Guessing, interrupted, restless*	
40	Memory for dot configurations	
	Guessing, restless, interrupted.	
41	Matching amount when configuration and color	

TOM D.

Chronological Age: Four years, six months.
Educational Training: Three months in nursery school.
Presenting Problem: Lethargic, clumsy, has difficulty in keeping up with group intellectually and socially.

School Report

Tom is blond, rather tall for his age, a pleasant looking, blue-eyed boy. He is a little clumsy and drools occasionally. Tom is the older of two children; his younger sister is about two years old. The mother is pregnant and decided to send Tom to the nursery school. She is a high school graduate and stays home to take care of the family. She worked before her marriage as a secretary. The father is a truck driver. English is spoken at home. The mother reported that Tom started to walk by himself at about twelve to fourteen months and to say more than "mama" and "dada" at about two years. His speech is not yet clear. Reportedly, he is a happy, good natured, quiet child. In the nursery school he presents no problem but is rather shy and withdrawn, requiring a lot of personal attention from the teacher to get him to work or join a group. He works poorly, lacks energy, is lethargic, and lacks initiative in play. If not directed often, he will sit doing nothing. Children do not care for him but will accept him if an adult requests them to include him.

Evaluation

Physical Functioning and Sensory Status

Tom responded adequately to visual and auditory stimuli. He had some difficulty in Item 4 (depth perception, binocularity) which may be due to his clumsiness and slight tremor; the position most difficult for him was diagonal. He is a clumsy, poorly coordinated child; fine manipulative skills are poor (cannot button, cannot use scissors as expected, has difficulty catching ball, jumping). Tom had difficulty in Item 6 (competence in using two systems; using touch and vision together). He looked as if he was unable to understand what he was supposed to do. He benefited from Probe A with the circle, and once he was able to understand a task, he continued on his own.

Perceptual Functioning

Tom was able to match simple forms but confused those that are more complex (Item 9). He did well when choice was reduced, and with help he gradually discriminated better. He could match some colors but got confused with dark ones (purple, blue, green). When the task was repeated he succeeded. Tom became confused if he had to sustain attention (Item 14), because he was distracted, and his performance deteriorated. To succeed, Tom needed constant guidance. He had no difficulty with Probe A; he distinguished the circle, square, triangle, and cross. He confused the square and triangle with the diamond when presented in Item 9. Tom put parts together only following demonstration, not after verbal instruction. He was unable to put together the four-part circle (Item 15); even with additional demonstrations he struggled with the last part.

Tom's pencil grasp was poor. He scribbled spontaneously and willingly (i.e., "coloring"). He was able to imitate lines and drew a poorly controlled circle. With sticks he imitated only one; often he was confused and started to play. He imitated a bridge (Probe B, Item 17). He liked to play with blocks, but only stacking them over and over or putting the blocks in a box, or lining them up ("trains").

Competence in Learning for Short-Term Retention

Tom sat quietly but seemed to concentrate poorly. He was able to recognize forms when they were concretized for him and additionally demonstrated (Probe B, Item 18). He looked for hidden toys. He was able to repeat two digits but mostly only one word, and once a two-word phrase. He seemed less attentive with verbal tasks. For Items 23 and 24 he showed no comprehension; he indiscriminately clapped his hands, and he drew a circle, but did not imitate the correct pattern.

Language Competence

As checked Tom understood naming and simple descriptions. He had difficulty indicating big and little and did it with some hesitancy in the concrete situation (Probe A, Item 29—spoons). He was unable to follow more complex verbal commands; he followed only one command, and that in a concrete situation. To describe pictures he used single words and needed a lot of prodding. He did not enumerate spontaneously. He answered questions in a monosyllabic way or by a short sentence. His articulation was poor, but speech was mostly intelligible.

Cognitive Functioning

Most tests were not given because they were evidently beyond his level. On Item 37, Tom was able to give one block on request and for two he gave more than one but not the correct number. He counted a little from memory but did not touch the corresponding block. For amount recognition (Item 38) he was unaware of the task; he randomly placed a "row" of pennies.

Educational Planning

Functioning level: Low level of functioning indicates need for full medical and psychological work-up.

Essential ingredients to be considered in educational prescription:

1. Quiet, compliant, tries when requested. Learns better from demonstrations than verbal instructions.
2. Relatively good in simple matching, discriminating, naming.
3. Tasks presented to him should be simple, choice limited; verbalization simple; guidance step-by-step.
4. Enjoys success; needs very easy work to build his self confidence.
5. Poor motor control and coordination; poor pencil grasp; needs exercises for motor control and coordination.
6. Drools occasionally, poorly articulated speech, and verbalization monosyllabic. Needs stimulation of simple conversation.
7. Comprehension limited all over. Level should be set low. Shy, quiet, prone to withdraw, passive, lethargic. He needs encouragement and guidance to be occupied.
8. The desirability of special class placement should be explored.

Name __Tom D.__ Sex __M__ D.O.B. _____ Age __4-6__ School __Nursery__

Date of Test _____

PSYCHOEDUCATIONAL EVALUATION
OF THE PRESCHOOL CHILD

Item No.	Name of Item or Probe	Observations and Teaching Suggestions

SECTION I. PHYSICAL FUNCTIONING AND SENSORY STATUS

Item No.	Name of Item or Probe	Observations and Teaching Suggestions
1 —	Manual dexterity _poor, awkward, drools_	_Medical attention — vision? motor difficulties?._
2 +	Visual acuity	_More physical exercises- ball games, gymnastics, use of scissors or pencil, stringing beads, etc._
3 +	Visual pursuit	
4 —	Depth perception, binocularity _Comprehension problem? Awkwardness or vision?_	
5 +	Auditory acuity	
—	Probe A: Simplify task	
6 —	Using touch and vision together _Comprehension problem? Awkward._	
+	Probe A. Make task concrete	

SECTION II. PERCEPTUAL FUNCTIONING

Item No.	Name of Item or Probe	Observations and Teaching Suggestions
7 —	Color matching _Some success, difficulty with darks - confused blue, purple, green._	
+	Probe A. Reduce choices	
8 +	Matching of solid forms on white background	
—	Probe A. Make task concrete	
—	Probes B and C. Reduce choices and make concrete	

83

Item No.	Name of Item or Probe	Observations and Teaching Suggestions
	Probe D. Tactile and kinesthetic stimuli	
	Probe E. Use of formboard	
9 ———	Matching of small outline forms	*Confuses diamond, square + triangle*
)	Probe A. Reduce choices	
)	Probe B. Tactile and kinesthetic stimuli	
+	Probe C. Reduce choices further	*Give more experience at this level.*
10)	Recognition of configuration of dots	*Simple matching of forms and colors. Slowly increase complexity. Try matching of pictures in "lotto" game.*
)	Probe A. Reduce choices	*Totally confused, became quite restless*
)	Probe B. Demonstrate	
11 ———	Matching of numbers and word configurations	
	Probe A. Reduce choices	
	Probe B. Make task concrete	
	Probe C. Match letter symbols	
12 ———	Fitting two halves of a circle on request	*Difficulty in following verbal commands — Poor comprehension*
+	Probe A. Demonstrate	*Practice verbal guidance of action.*
	Probe B. Fit halves of picture	
	Probe C. Move one piece	
13 +	Fitting two halves of a square after demonstration and verbal description	

Item No.	Name of Item or Probe	Observations and Teaching Suggestions
14	Visual matching of a patterned arrangement of forms	*Performance deteriorates – distracted.*
+		
	Probe A. Reduce choices	
——	Probe B. Simplify and make task concrete	
15	Fitting four quarters of a circle after demonstration and verbal description	
∫		
	Probe A. Tactile and kinesthetic stimuli	
—	Probe B. Make task concrete	*Erratic, tires easily*
16	Visually guided hand movements; copy design with a pencil	*Poor pencil grasp, scribbles spontaneously.* *Encourage use of pencil, chalk.*
—		
	Probe A. Simplify designs	*Imitates lines accurately – circle inadequately* *Start with lines and circle, finger-painting and coloring.*
—	Probe B. Tactile and kinesthetic stimuli	
17	Construction of stick designs from model	*Responded by playing. Could only imitate one.*
∫		
	Probe A. Simplify designs	
+	Probe B. Three-block construction	
——	Probe C. Build a tower	
——	Probe D. Observe block play	

Item No.	Name of Item or Probe	Observations and Teaching Suggestions

SECTION III. COMPETENCE IN LEARNING FOR SHORT-TERM RETENTION

Item No.	Name of Item or Probe	Observations and Teaching Suggestions
18	— Delayed recognition of large solid forms	
	— Probe A. Reduce choices	
	+ Probe B. Make task concrete	
	Probe C. Tactile and kinesthetic stimuli	
19	= Delayed recognition of small outline forms	
	— *Distracted.*	
	— Probe A. Reduce choices	
20	≡ Recall of missing picture from memory	*Difficulty in concentrating. Recalls 2 words or digits. Enjoys hidden toy games.*
	— Probe A. Make task concrete	
	+ Probe B. Simplify task	
21	= Repetition of digits	
22	— Repetition of words, phrases, and sentences *1 word well. Only 1 of three 2-word phrases.*	
23	= Repetition of spaced sounds *clapped hands, no pattern*	
24	= Memory for spaced circles *Confused, copied one circle.*	
	— Probe A. Simplify task	
	— Probe B. Make task concrete	

Item No.	Name of Item or Probe	Observations and Teaching Suggestions

SECTION IV. LANGUAGE COMPETENCE

25 ✝	Identification of pictures of familiar objects when named	*Encourage speech – at start, through naming objects and asking simple questions*
26 ✝	Recognition of pictures of objects when described in terms of use	*Give one verbal command.*
	Probe A. Make task concrete	*Support language and comprehension by demonstration, pictures, gestures.*
	Probe B. Reduce choices	
	Probe C. Focus child's attention	
27 ✝	Recognition of described action in pictures	
28 ✝	Recognition of "night" and "day" when named in pictures	
29 —	Recognition of size differences in circles	
✝	Probe A. Make task concrete	*Guessed?*
	Probe B. Use familiar objects	
30 —	Identification of colors when named	
—	Probe A. Reduce choices	
✝	Probe B. Color matching	*(See item 7)*
31 —	Obeying simple commands	*Follows one command*
✝	Probe A. Use familiar toy	

Item No.	Name of Item or Probe	Observations and Teaching Suggestions
32	Story comprehension; ability to select pertinent pictures	
	Probe A. Simplify task	
33	Responding to named spatial relations	*Not at all – Only responded to last word. Discontinued.*
34	Use of words to label and define	*Monosyllabic, poor articulation, needs prodding to name – No spontaneous enumerations.*
35	Quality of sentence structure in guided speech; response to pictures and questions	*Naming only, responds to questions with one word, phrase – "bus", "play ball"*

SECTION V. COGNITIVE FUNCTIONING

Item No.	Name of Item or Probe	Observations and Teaching Suggestions
36	Grading of sizes in small outline circles	*Not given*
	Probe A. Demonstrate and make concrete	*Number concepts not developed. Some counting by rote, not related sequentially to objects "counted"*
	Probe B. Reduce choices	
	Probe C. Grading to standard	*Merely played – erratic*
37	Amount concept	
	Probe A. Additional trial –	*only "one"*
38	Amount recognition	*Not aware of meaning of matching – puts objects in row.*
39	Finding numbers and words from memory after short exposure	
40	Memory for dot configurations	
41	Matching amount when configuration and color differ	

88

Appendix II

Test Materials Not Supplied

This list of materials is an inventory of the kinds of items that are readily available to a classroom preschool teacher. In keeping with the philosophy of this manual, these specific materials are not indispensable; substitutions are often quite appropriate. The object is not the crucial matter. For example, with Item 24, examiners usually use six pennies or blocks, but toy cars or dolls may also be used.

Item 1: chalk, board, paper, crayon or pencil, peg board and pegs.
Item 2: 4 toys (car, ball, cup, doll, animal, etc.) and matching pictures.
Item 3: flashlight.
Item 4: drinking straw, pointer stick.
Item 5: 3 plastic pill vials, salt, rice, clips.
Item 14, Probe B: doll.
Item 17: cardboard shield and matchsticks. *Probe B:* 8 blocks.

Item 20, Probe A: brush and comb, shoe, spoon. *Probe B:* 3 boxes or paper cups, toy animal, shield.
Item 24: red crayon, paper. *Probe B:* 6 pennies or 6 toy cars or dolls.
Item 26, Probe A: brush and comb, spoon, shoe, cup.
Item 29, Probe A: 2 teaspoons, 1 doll spoon, *Probe B:* 2 tablespoons, 2 teaspoons.
Item 31: pencil, book, car.
Item 37: 10 pennies.
Item 38: 30 pennies or chips.

Appendix III

Test Material Patterns

On the following pages are the test material patterns to be used in administering the Main Items and Probes.

Cut out the cards along the dotted lines. To ensure their durability in repeated use, the cards can be pasted onto sturdy cardboard. For storage of the cut-out materials, use clasp envelopes marked with each Item number or Probe letter for easy identification.

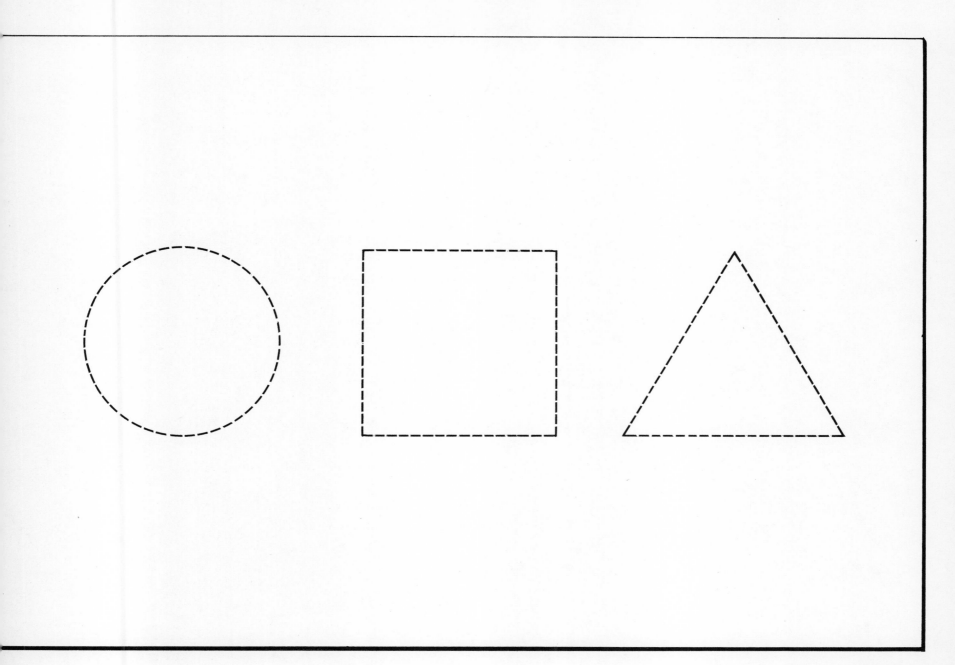

| red | red | yellow | yellow | blue | blue |

| green | green | orange | orange | purple | purple |

Main Item 7

Main Item 9

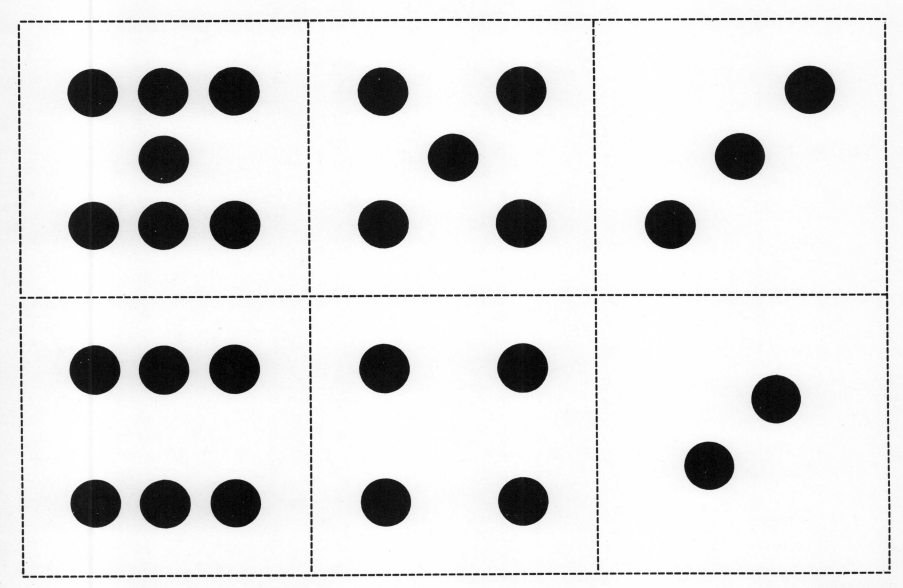

Main Item 10
Main Item 40

(continued on next page)

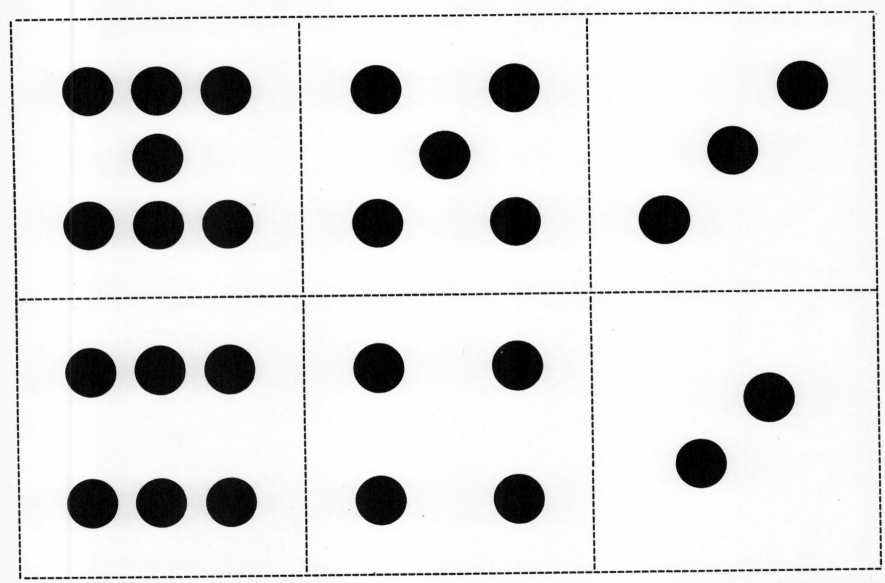

Main Item 10
Main Item 40

(continued on next page)

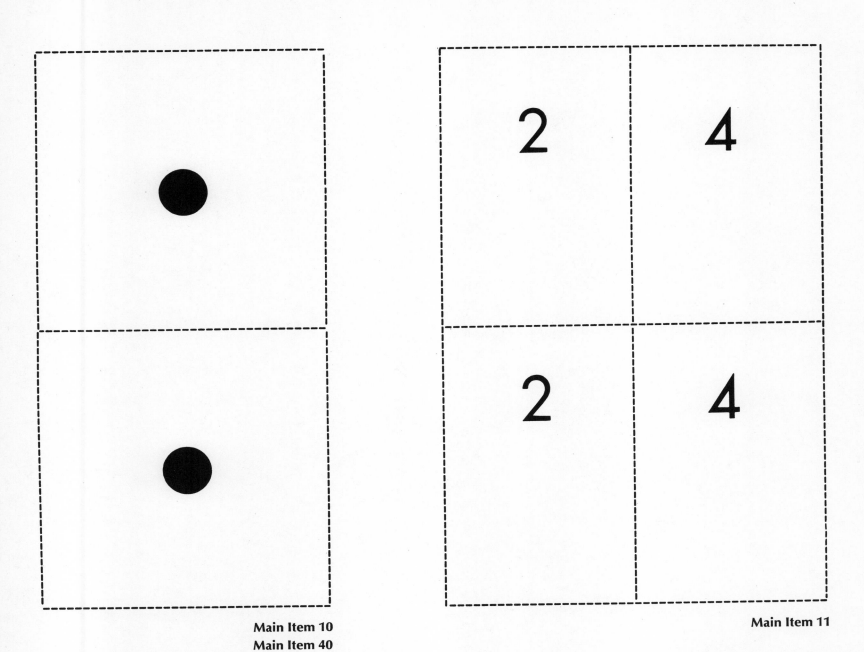

Main Item 10
Main Item 40

Main Item 11

(continued on next page)

home	cat	tac	sat
home	cat	tac	sat

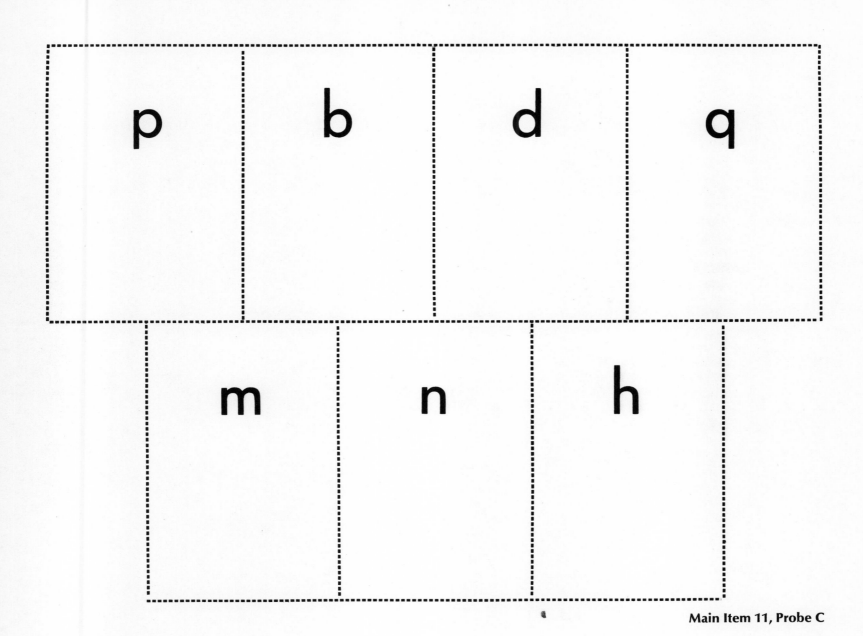

Main Item 11, Probe C

(continued on next page)

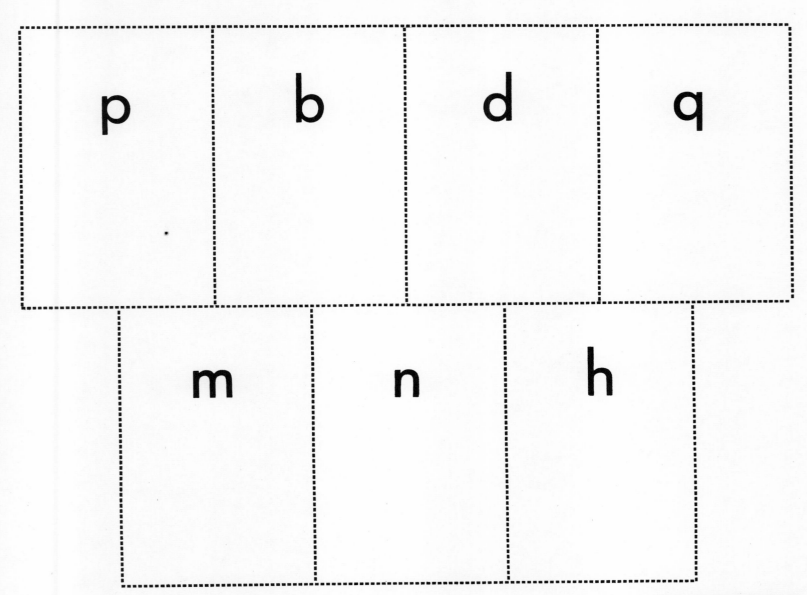

Main Item 11, Probe C

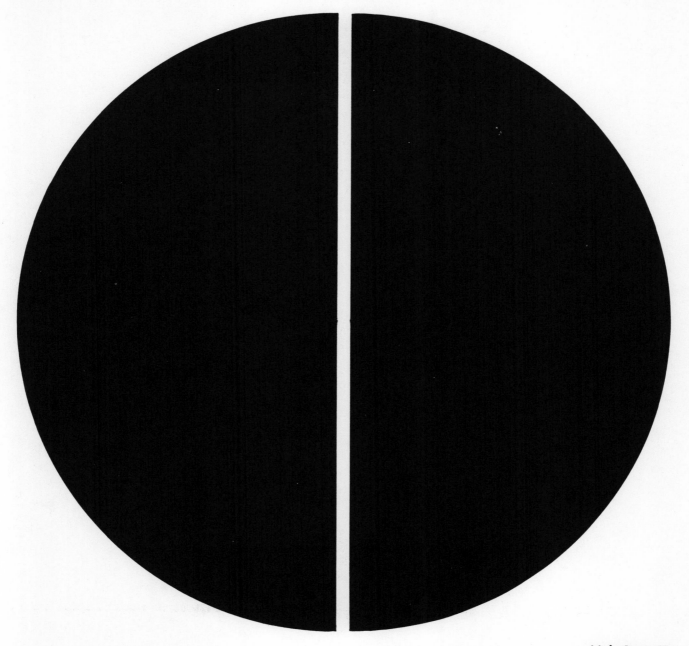

Main Item 12

Main Item 12, Probe B

Main Item 13

Main Item 14

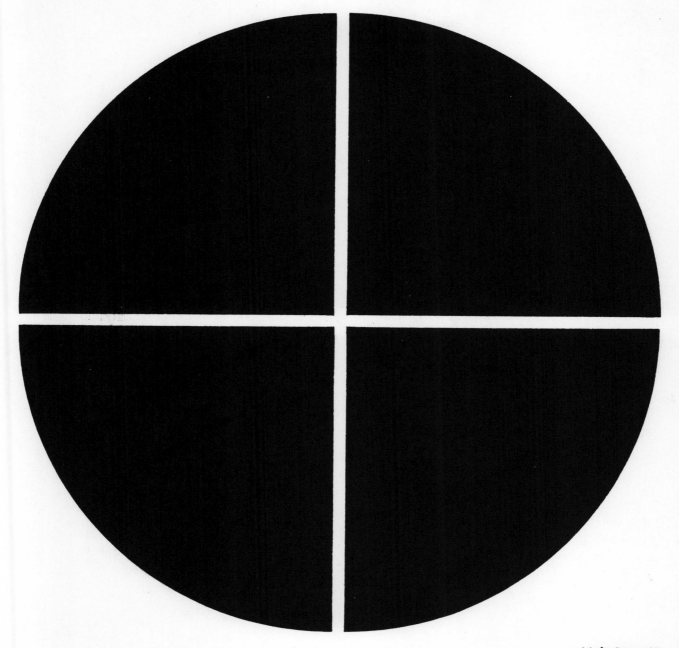

Main Item 15

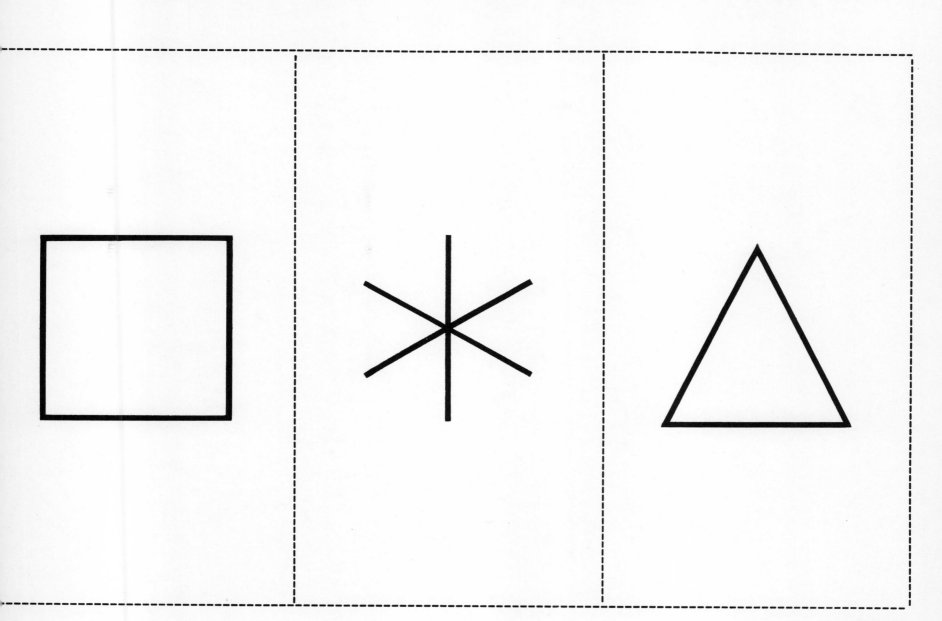

Main Item 16, Probe A

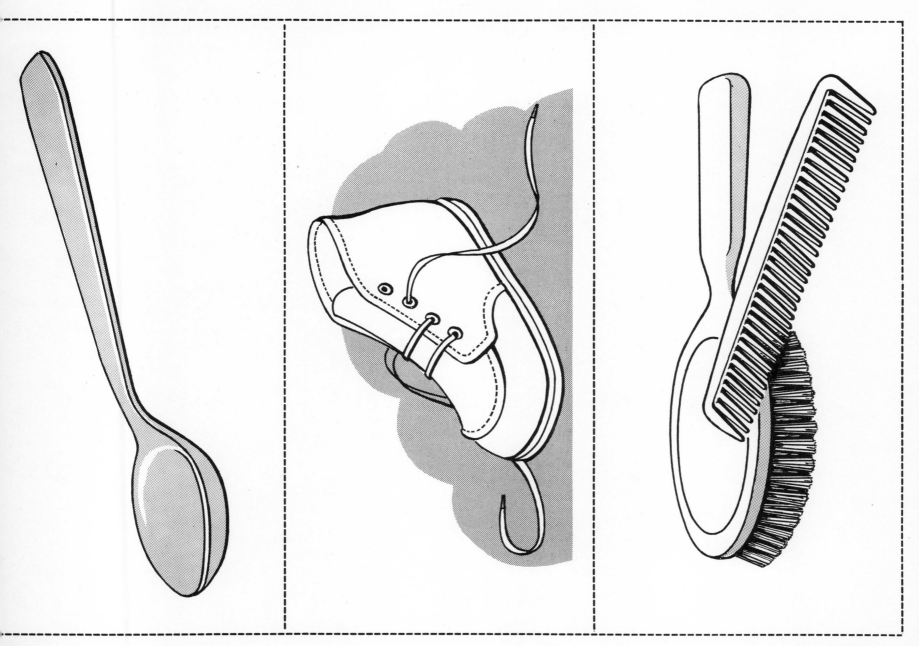

Main Item 27

Main Item 28

(continued on next page)

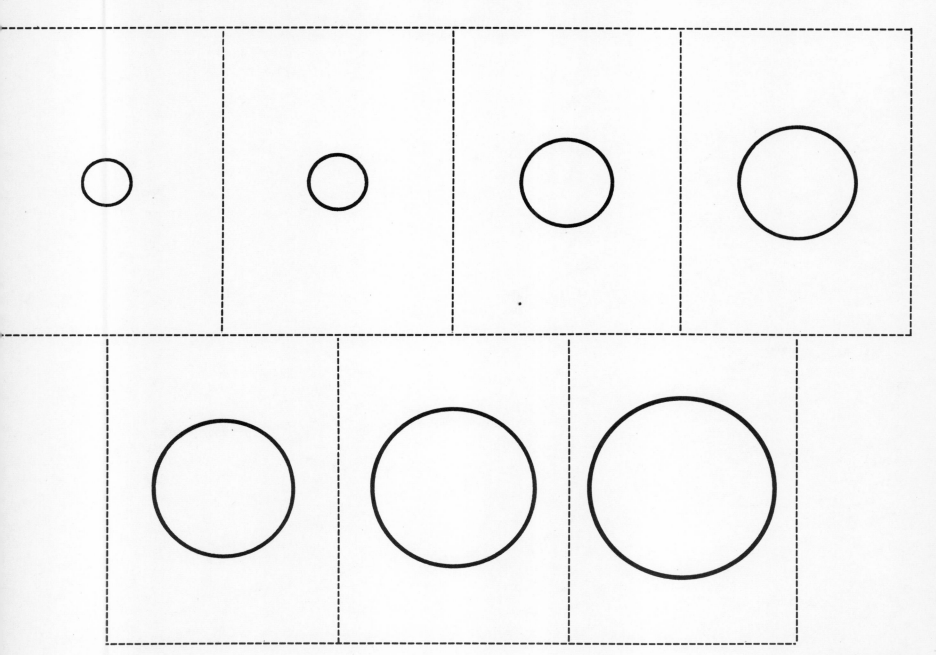

Main Item 29

Main Item 36

Goldilocks and the Three Bears

Once upon a time there lived three bears. Papa Bear was very big. Mama Bear was middle-sized. And Baby Bear was small.

One day Mama Bear made some oatmeal. "It smells good!" she said.

"It looks good!" said Baby Bear.

"But it's too hot," finished Papa Bear. "Let's take a walk while it cools." And away they went.

Pretty soon a little girl came down the path. Her name was Goldilocks. "I wonder who lives here," she thought. "I think I'll stop to visit." She went inside, and there were the three bowls of oatmeal on the table. "It looks so good, I'm going to try it," she said.

But the Papa Bear's oatmeal was much too hot. Mama Bear's oatmeal was too cold. Goldilocks tasted Baby Bear's oatmeal and it was just right! She ate it all up!

"Now," she thought, "I'll sit down and wait for them to come home." First she sat in Papa Bear's big chair, but that was too hard. Then she tried Mama Bear's middle-sized chair, but that was too soft. Then she tried Baby Bear's tiny chair. It was just right! Goldilocks sat down in it, and it broke into many pieces.

Goldilocks was very sleepy. She went up to the bedroom. There was Papa Bear's big, wide bed. Goldilocks lay down on it, but it was too hard. Then she tried Mama Bear's middle-sized bed, but that was so soft she could hardly see up over the quilts. Last of all, she tried Baby Bear's tiny bed. Do you know, it was just right! It felt so good that Goldilocks went to sleep. And while she slept, the three bears came home.

Papa Bear went right to his big bowl. He growled, "Someone has been tasting my oatmeal!"

"Someone tasted mine too!" said Mama Bear, as she peeked into her middle-sized bowl.

Baby Bear picked up his tiny bowl. "Someone ate my oatmeal—all of it!" he squeaked in his little bear voice.

"And look here," said Papa Bear. "Someone has been sitting in my big chair."

"And in my middle-sized chair," said Mama Bear.

"Oh, oh," squeaked Baby Bear. "Someone has broken my tiny chair all to pieces!"

Then they went upstairs. "Someone's been lying on my big bed!" growled Papa Bear.

"And on my middle-sized bed," said Mama Bear.

"Oh, look," squeaked Baby Bear, with a very loud squeak. "Someone's been lying on my bed—and *she's still here!*"

Just then Goldilocks woke up. She saw the three bears standing there beside the bed. With one jump she was at the top of the stairs. And with another jump she was downstairs, running just as fast as she could.

"Come back!" shouted the three bears. "We want to be friends."

But Goldilocks kept running. And it was a long, long time before she went walking that way again.

Main Item 32

(continued on next page)

Main Item 32

(continued on next page)

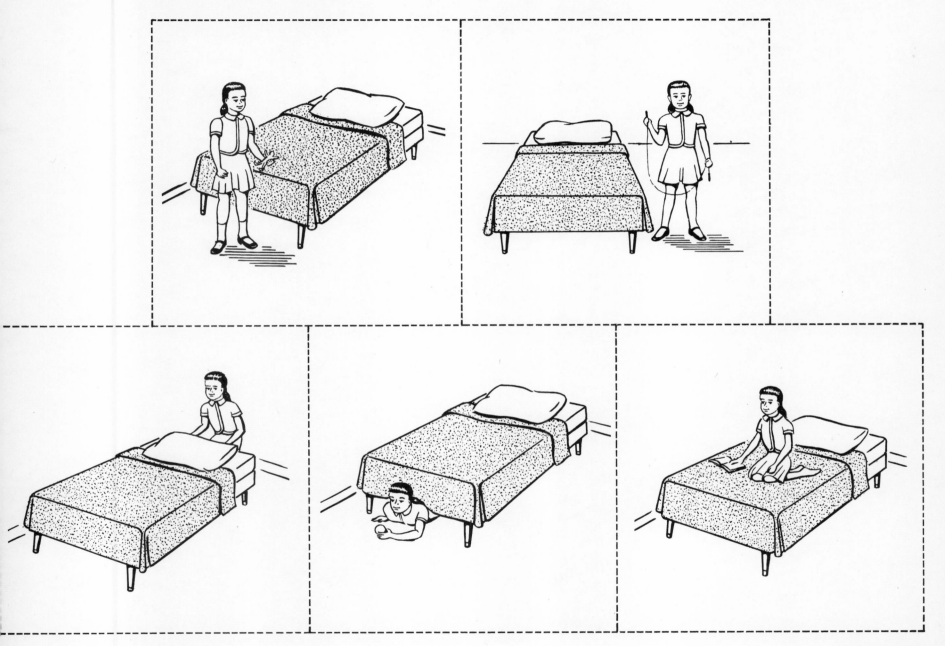

Main Item 33

(continued on next page)

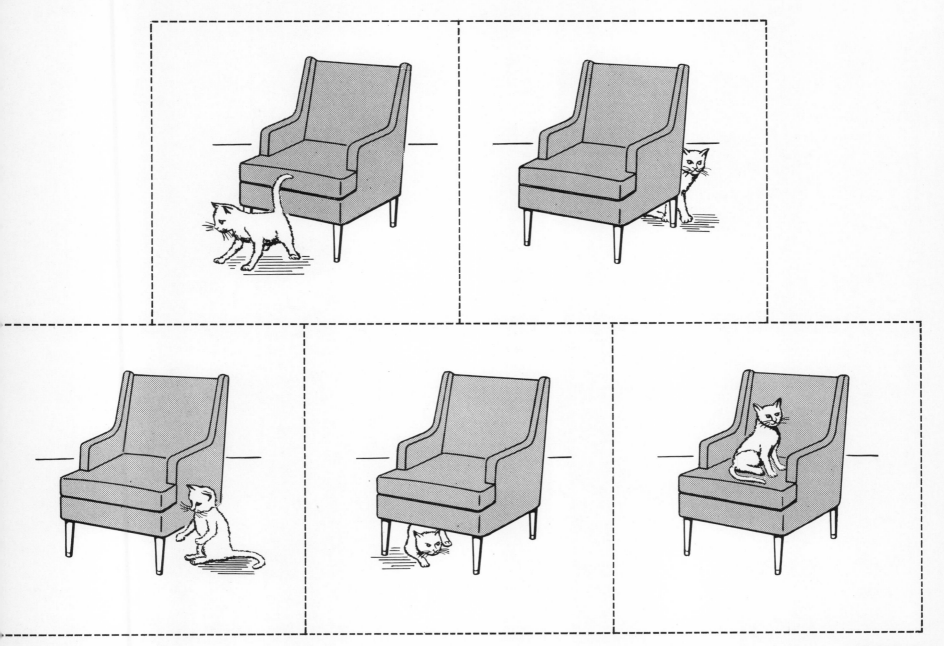

Main Item 33

Main Item 35

Main Item 36, Probe C

(continued on next page)

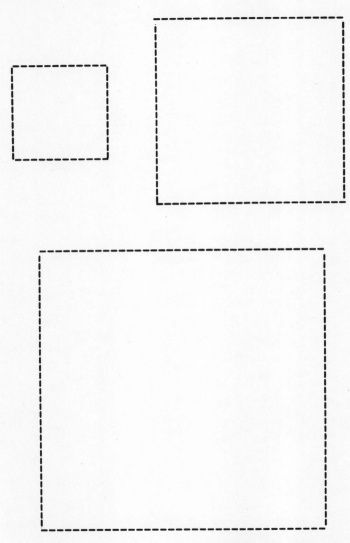

Main Item 36, Probe C

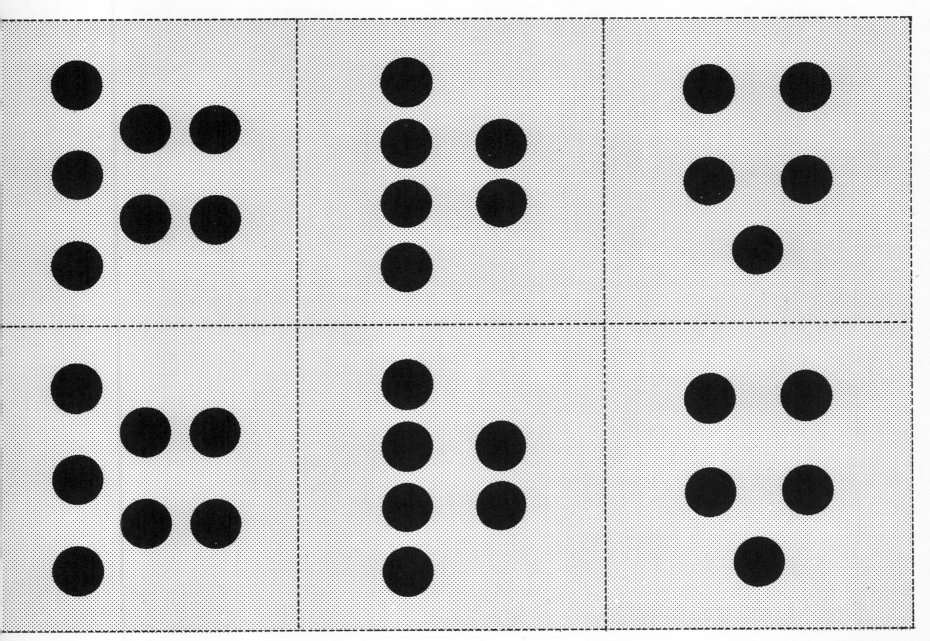